LUCKY RICE

CLARKSON POTTER/
PUBLISHERS

NEW YORK

LUCKY RICE

STORES *and* RECIPES
from NIGHT MARKETS, FEASTS,
and FAMILY TABLES

DANIELLE CHANG

Photographs by Christina Holmes

Published in the United States by Clarkson Potter/
Publishers, an imprint of the Crown Publishing Group,
a division of Penguin Random House LLC, New York.
www.crownpublishing.com
www.clarksonpotter.com

CLARKSON POTTER is a trademark and POTTER with
colophon is a registered trademark of Penguin Random
House LLC.

Library of Congress Cataloging-in-Publication Data
Chang, Danielle
    Lucky rice / Danielle Chang.—First edition.
        pages   cm
    1. Cooking, Asian.   I. Title.
    TX724.5.A1C4245 2016
    641.595—dc23   2015004859

ISBN 978-0-8041-8668-1
eBook ISBN 978-0-8041-8669-8

Printed in China

Book and cover design by Danielle Deschenes
Endpaper pattern by Shutterstock © Iuliia Grankina

10 9 8 7 6 5 4 3 2 1

First Edition

TO MY DAUGHTERS, COLETTE
AND CLARISSA, WHO HAVE
TAUGHT ME THAT A SIMPLE BOWL
OF RICE BECOMES A FEAST WHEN
SHARED IN THE COMPANY OF
THOSE YOU CHERISH.

CONTENTS

While growing up in Carmichael, California, I lived with my grandfather and grandmother, H.T. and Lien Ling, who were both immigrants from Hong Kong. Grandma served up nightly meals such as fried rice with Chinese *lap cheong* (sausage), handmade won ton soup, braised meat dishes, congee with ham hock, and various kinds of stir-fry. Oh, what I would do for a taste of one of her dishes now!

To support their family, Lien and H.T. worked in a restaurant and Lien taught piano lessons on the side. After years of saving, our family finally opened the first Chinese restaurant in Folsom, California, called Hop Sing. It catered to a non-Chinese crowd—nothing "too exotic" my grannie told me. The restaurant was so popular that people would come from all over the Sacramento area to have dinner there.

Six decades later, Chinese restaurants are ubiquitous in America, with hundreds that feature region-specific dishes: spicy Hunanese stews, bold Sichuanese *ma po* tofu, Beijing-style hot pots, and more. More and more cities are getting Japanese *izakaya* restaurants and Korean BBQ joints, too. Today, Asian food in America means so much more than Egg Foo Young or sushi.

While cohosting the ABC daytime talk show *The View*, more than a decade ago, I met Danielle Chang, who was then the publisher of the lifestyle magazine *Simplycity*. Born in Taiwan and raised in Palo Alto, Danielle always dreamed of creating a platform to celebrate Asian culture. At one time, the two of us even entertained wild notions of starting an Asian lifestyle magazine, but we decided that it wasn't the right time. Danielle, however, never let go of her dream. She realized instead that the best way to open the door to the richness of Asia and its people would be through its food.

After more than six years since first launching her LUCKYRICE food festival, Danielle presents this delicious cookbook. In the following pages, you'll read incredible stories about cooking and dining traditions and get recipes from across Asia that would be right at home in kitchens from San Francisco to Charleston. It's too bad my grannie isn't around anymore; not only would her *lap cheong* fried rice have been a serious contender for *Lucky Rice*, but also I know she'd be so pleased to see many classics and new creations collected in a beautiful cookbook for a new generation of Americans. How lucky are we!

★ LISA LING

S picy tacos stuffed with bulgogi and fermented kimchi, gingery Japanese-style fried chicken, bright and frothy bubble teas . . . these are the delicious new classics that have breached the culinary borders between Asia and the rest of the world. More and more, we're sitting down together to enjoy bowls of rice rather than to break bread. As our hunger for and curiosity about Asian food intensify, our repertoire is no longer limited to fortune cookies, take-out Chinese, and California rolls.

We're not just becoming more adventurous eaters; we're also more knowledgeable about Asian culture. We see that the largest continent is not just one monolith of chopsticks and soy sauce but rather a collection of interwoven yet disparate cultures and cuisines. Ten years ago, for instance, when take-out menus still lumped Thai, Chinese, and Japanese dishes into one cuisine, if I told people that I was born in Taiwan, many would then innocently regale me with stories of their Thailand vacations. But not anymore, and I like to think it's because our bellies have taught us well.

Suddenly, the traditional foods that I grew up eating—dishes like pho, soup dumplings, and collagen-rich bone broths—are comforting a new sophisticated generation of food enthusiasts, professional chefs, and home cooks who enjoy approaching other cultures through the local food. Some of the most in-demand chefs have rewarded our quest for new food adventures by weaving such traditional spices and flavors as numbing Sichuanese peppercorns and pungent Vietnamese fish sauce into their otherwise non-Asian menus—and in the process creating a bold new cuisine. Asian cuisine has never been more relevant than it is today.

When I was a child, my family and I lived on a crooked street called Jing Jang Jie in old Taipei. Our aunts and uncles occupied the floors below and above us, and the family business was conveniently located on the ground floor. Our days always revolved around food. I'd wake to the sound of a street food vendor, the bell on his cart ringing to announce the arrival of *you tiao* (a fried Chinese doughnut) along with the fresh soybean milk that we would dip the "doughnuts" into. At night, when we gathered for dinner, a certain melodic rhythm developed from the click-clacking of the chopsticks, the spinning of the lazy Susan, and the shared activity of sip, slurp, swallow. Each family member played their part differently: my Aunt

Vanessa would take her time, chewing slowly and conscientiously, while my Uncle Eric would swallow his food whole and take command of the lazy Susan, spinning it quickly so that his favorite dishes would land right under his nose.

When I was five, our family moved to Houston, Texas. Until then, I had never had a hot dog or French fries and I could barely speak a lick of English. I was that new girl who brought chicken feet and stewed eggs on rice in her lunchbox instead of PB&J sandwiches. In my struggle to assimilate, I fought to forget my Chinese heritage, pretending not to speak the language and opting for pizza instead of dim sum. The irony that I have subsequently created LUCKYRICE, a multi-city festival that celebrates Asian food, is not lost on my parents and me; bridging the two cultures of my childhood has been a lofty yet life-long aspiration of mine.

Eager to share cultural stories through the lens of food and drink, I set up the food festival LUCKYRICE in New York in 2010. Momentum for learning more about Asian cuisine was already building, but a platform didn't yet exist for sharing our enthusiasm and pushing the conversation forward. Soon we took the festival on the road, bringing festivities like night markets, mock Chinese wedding banquets, ramen slurpfests, and epicurean cocktail feasts to Miami, Toronto, San Francisco, and even underneath the Manhattan Bridge in Brooklyn. In traveling the country, we've been lucky to work with our culinary heroes: celebrated chefs, some Asian and some not, as well as their protégés, who are impacting this cuisine. Though many of these recipes are inspired by those chefs and their innovative dishes as well as dishes I grew up with, they are all my own—developed through years of cooking for family and friends.

As with the festivals, my hope is that this cookbook will bring alive the colorful dishes of Korea, the wide range of Chinese cooking techniques, and the distinctions among various Indian spices. The book hops around Asia, and what you'll find is not an encyclopedia of all of its food, but rather a curated selection of enduring recipes and newer favorites that feed our current obsession with Asian cuisine. Try any of them. I promise that they are all are delicious, and with any luck, they'll stoke your appetite for more.

STREET EATS

TAIWANESE BEEF
NOODLE SOUP

Page 31

Whether you're in Tokyo, Ho Chi Minh City, or Taipei, ask locals where to go for the best food and you will often hear the refrain "night markets." If street food is the lifeblood of Asian culinary culture, then night markets are its heartbeat. Similar to a European piazza, where folks while away their evening over conversation and food, night markets are where you go for what's known as *xiao ye*, or "late-night eats."

There's a Chinese phrase, *re nao*, which translates literally to "hot and noisy" but has no true English equivalent. In fact, night markets are nothing if not *re nao*; the spectacle of a night market assaults your senses on every level. Perhaps that is part of the appeal—the commotion of the crowds, the J-pop–inspired teenagers sharing Bubble Tea (page 74), even the wrinkled old men with missing teeth (from years of chewing betel nut) munching on Barbecued Squid-on-a-Stick (page 18).

In Ho Chi Minh City, you'll find hordes of motorcycles parked next to people slurping down bowls of pho. In Hong Kong, where shopping is a nonstop sport, the food stalls in the local Mongkok neighborhood allow you to nourish yourself with Taiwanese Beef Noodle Soup (page 31) while you satisfy your lust for knock-off Vuitton. Street food may be cheap and cheerful, but it's also a serious craft and a culinary tradition that's been passed down through generations. In Singapore, for example, night markets are home to highly competitive hawkers selling dishes like Curry *Laksa* (page 21) and Beef Satay (opposite). There might be ten stalls in a row all selling the same dish, and fistfights often break out over whose is the best. (Hint: It's the stall with the longest line.)

When we held our first LUCKYRICE Festival Night Market back in 2010, we set out to re-create the celebratory frenzy of the ones in Asia, but with a local Brooklyn flavor. We brought in nearly fifty of our favorite street food vendors, and one of the chefs from Taiwan decided to serve stinky tofu to complete the experience; so our festivity was blessed with the sights, sounds—and, yes, smells—of a true night market. Since that first event, the Night Market has gone on to become our most popular LUCKYRICE event and the culture of night markets has spread across the country, so now you can experience the tastes of Taiwan or Thailand without a passport.

BEEF SATAY

MAKES 32 SKEWERS, SERVES ABOUT 8 AS AN APPETIZER

To me, the perfect street eat is something that you can hold in one hand, and meat-on-a-stick, or satay, certainly fits the bill. Though you'll find a variety of meats in night markets (lamb is popular in Beijing, while offal like chicken hearts and livers is prized in Japanese yakitori), traditional satay is made with either chicken or beef. This one is based on an Indonesian recipe, and features charred yet tender steak, made even more mouthwatering when dipped in a nutty, creamy sauce. For the authentic street food flavor, a charcoal grill is best, but a gas grill or even an indoor stovetop grill pan works, too.

PREPARE THE BEEF: Cut the meat into ⅛-inch-thick strips, each about 1 inch wide and 6 inches long. (Freezing the meat for about 15 minutes beforehand will make it easier to slice.)

In a large bowl, combine the lime juice, soy sauce, fish sauce, honey, garlic, ginger, coriander, and cumin. Add the steak strips and toss to coat in the marinade. Cover with plastic wrap and refrigerate for at least 1 hour and up to a day.

MAKE THE SAUCE: Using a mortar and pestle (or a food processor), pound the peanuts until coarsely chopped; then transfer them to a small bowl and set aside. Pound the shallots, lemongrass, ginger, garlic, and chile together with the mortar and pestle or add to the food processor and pulse until coarsely blended.

Heat the vegetable oil in a medium pot. Add the shallot mixture and stir-fry until it is browned and fragrant, about 3 minutes. Add the coarsely ground peanuts, coconut milk, honey, fish sauce, and 1 cup of water. Bring to a boil, reduce the heat, and simmer, stirring occasionally, until the sauce thickens, about 5 minutes.

recipe continues

FOR THE MEAT SKEWERS:

1½ pounds **rump roast steak**

2 tablespoons fresh **lime juice**

2 tablespoons **soy sauce**

2 tablespoons **fish sauce**

2 tablespoons **honey**

4 **garlic cloves**, minced

1 tablespoon finely chopped fresh **ginger**

1 teaspoon ground **coriander**

1 teaspoon ground **cumin**

FOR THE PEANUT SAUCE:

½ cup **unsalted roasted peanuts**

½ cup **shallots**, chopped

1 **lemongrass stalk**, trimmed and chopped

1 tablespoon grated fresh **ginger**

2 **garlic cloves**, chopped

1 fresh **red Thai chile**, seeded and stemmed

1 tablespoon **vegetable oil**

½ cup **coconut milk**

1 tablespoon **honey**

2 tablespoons **fish sauce**

Salt and freshly **ground black pepper** to taste

Lime wedges, for serving

Meanwhile, soak 32 six-inch wooden skewers in a bowl of warm water for about 10 minutes.

Remove the meat from the marinade and discard the marinade. Thread each slice of marinated meat onto a skewer so that it is undulating like a ribbon. Season with salt and pepper.

Heat a grill and oil the grate. Grill the satay in batches until the beef is just medium-rare, about 2 minutes on each side. Serve with the sauce for dipping and the lime wedges for squeezing over each skewer.

BARBECUED
SQUID-ON-A-STICK
Page 18

GRILLED CHICKEN
TSUKUNE SAUSAGE
Page 19

BEEF SATAY
Page 15

BARBECUED SQUID-ON-A-STICK

Ikayaki

SERVES 8 (1 SQUID PER PERSON)

Grilled squid is as much a favorite in Asia as hot dogs are in America—served outside movie theaters, at temples, and of course at night markets. I grew up loving this chewy, briny, everyday treat that's popular from Kyoto, Japan, to Beijing, China. I like to serve this along with other grilled things like Beef Satay (page 15) or *Dango* (page 146)—a perfect spread for a summer barbecue.

8 whole **fresh squid** (bodies and tentacles)
½ cup **soy sauce**
¼ cup **mirin**
¼ cup **sake**
3 tablespoons **sugar**
Vegetable oil, for greasing the grill pan

Remove and discard the head of each squid, leaving the tentacles and body intact. Remove and discard the transparent bone and thin membrane from inside each squid body, and then make small centimeter-long cuts across the body, taking care to keep the body intact. Chop the tentacles in half. Place the squid pieces in a medium bowl.

To make the marinade, combine the soy sauce, mirin, and sake in a small saucepan. Place the pan over low heat, add the sugar, and stir until the sugar has dissolved, about 2 minutes. Let the mixture cool briefly, and then pour it over the squid. Cover and let sit for about 30 minutes in the refrigerator. Meanwhile, soak 8 wooden skewers in a bowl of warm water for about 10 minutes.

Remove the squid from the marinade and thread each body onto a skewer. At the end of each skewer, add the halved tentacles, piercing through its thickest part.

Heat a grill pan or an outdoor grill and grease the pan or grate with oil. Cook the skewers on the grill pan for about 2 minutes on each side, or until the squid is starting to char. Serve immediately.

★ ★ NOTE

Making cuts along the body of the squid helps to cook it more quickly and evenly but also makes it easier to eat off a stick.

GRILLED CHICKEN *TSUKUNE* SAUSAGE

MAKES 12 SKEWERS

Closet-size yakitori stalls (so small and casual that you might eat stand-ing up) are part of the fabric of Japanese street food life. There you can order stick after stick of skewered chicken parts, including this *tsu-kune* sausage. *Yakitori* literally means "grilled chicken," and in yakitori chicken culture, organic (or *jidori*) chicken is freshly killed (usually mere hours before you eat it) so that the meat retains all of its flavor and texture without requiring refrigeration.

MAKE THE GLAZE: Combine the soy sauce, sake, mirin, and sugar in a small saucepan. Bring to a gradual boil, stirring constantly to melt the sugar, and cook until the liquid has the consistency of a denser teriyaki sauce. Set aside. Meanwhile, soak 12 five-inch wooden skewers in a bowl with warm water for about 10 minutes.

COOK THE MEATBALLS: Divide the ground chicken in half. In a skillet, cook half of the meat until it is no longer pink, about 2 minutes. Combine the raw and cooked chicken in a medium bowl, and add the chopped shiso leaves and scallions. Sprinkle with the sesame oil and miso paste, and use your hands to combine the ingredients. Grease your hands with additional sesame oil, and shape the chicken mixture into 3-inch oblong sausages, each about 1 inch thick. Insert a skewer into each sausage.

Preheat a grill pan over medium-high heat, and grease it with vegetable oil. Place the shaped sausages onto the pan and grill for about 5 minutes on each side, or until they are no longer pink on the inside and just browned on the outside. Brush glaze on the sausages and continue to grill for about a minute on each side. Before serving, feel free to add more glaze.

FOR THE TARE GLAZE:

2 tablespoons **soy sauce**

2 tablespoons **sake**

2 tablespoons **mirin**

1 tablespoon **sugar**

FOR THE CHICKEN MEATBALLS:

1 pound **ground chicken**

10 fresh **shiso leaves**, finely chopped

4 **scallions** (green and white parts), finely chopped

2 tablespoons **Asian sesame oil**, plus more for shaping the sausage

1 tablespoon **miso paste**

Vegetable oil, for greasing the grill pan

★ ★
NOTE

Pre-cooking some of the ground chicken helps to make a plumper, less dense sausage, since chicken meat tends to shrink when it cooks.

DANDAN NOODLES

SERVES 4 AS A MEAL, OR 6 AS A SNACK

The Chinese word *dandan* derives from the name of the pole that street vendors traditionally carried over their shoulders while hawking bowls of noodles to pedestrians. The pole had a basket on either end—one to hold the noodles and the other for the sauce. This common street food—which became known literally as "noodles carried on a pole"—originates from Sichuan province, where the air smells of Sichuanese peppercorns with hints of sesame, preserved cabbage, black vinegar, and chopped garlic—the essential ingredients of this bowl of simple perfection.

¼ cup **peanut oil**

2 teaspoons coarsely ground **Sichuanese peppercorns**, or to taste

¼ cup **preserved cabbage** (*tianjin*)

2 **garlic cloves**, chopped

2 tablespoons chopped fresh **ginger**

1 pound **ground pork**

Kosher salt and freshly **ground black pepper**

1 1-pound package **Chinese wheat flour noodles**

½ cup **chicken broth**

¼ cup **chili oil**

¼ cup **black vinegar**

¼ cup **soy sauce**

¼ cup **sesame paste**

½ cup **unsalted roasted peanuts**, chopped, for serving

4 **scallions** (green and white parts), chopped on the diagonal, for serving

Heat a large wok on high heat and swirl in the peanut oil. Add the Sichuanese peppercorns and fry until fragrant, about 1 minute. Add the preserved cabbage, garlic, and ginger and stir-fry until fragrant, about 2 minutes.

Season the pork with kosher salt and black pepper, add it to the wok, and cook, stirring with the back of a spoon to break up the bits, until the pork is browned, about 8 minutes.

Meanwhile, cook the noodles in a large pot of boiling water according to the package directions. Drain, and rinse under cold running water. Divide the noodles among 4 soup bowls or 6 snack bowls.

Stir the chicken broth, chili oil, black vinegar, soy sauce, and sesame paste into the wok. Continue to simmer, stirring occasionally, until the sauce thickens, about 10 minutes.

Pour the pork mixture evenly over the noodles in the bowls. Garnish with the peanuts and scallions, and give a stir to mix everything together before eating.

CURRY *LAKSA*

SERVES 4

Lotsa laksa? Yes, please. In Singapore, where hawker stalls are found everywhere from outdoor markets to air-conditioned indoor food courts, you'll find *laksa*, a curry-noodle soup that speaks of the multi-faceted culinary history of the city. My favorite time to eat *laksa?* For breakfast or for a late-night snack—or both, to bookend the day. There are two primary types of *laksa*: *curry laksa* (made with coconut milk) and *asam laksa* (a sour version made with fish paste and tamarind). Though I love both, this recipe is the more popular curry version.

In a small bowl, soak the dried chiles in warm water for about 30 minutes or until rehydrated.

Cook the noodles in a large pot of boiling water according to the package directions. Drain, and divide the noodles among 4 large soup bowls.

In a food processor or using a mortar and pestle, grind the shallots, turmeric, galangal, lemongrass, drained chiles, candlenuts, and *belacan* with 2 tablespoons of the vegetable oil until a smooth paste is formed.

In a large pot, heat the remaining 6 tablespoons oil over medium-high heat. Add the spice paste and sauté, stirring often, until the mixture is fragrant, 2 to 3 minutes. Pour in the shrimp stock and bring to a boil. Add the coconut milk, fish sauce, and tofu puffs. Bring back to a boil. Add the prawns and cook for 2 to 3 minutes, until they turn red.

Ladle the hot soup over the noodles in the bowls, dividing the prawns and tofu puffs among the bowls. Top with the eggs, bean sprouts, julienned cucumber, and sliced lime leaves. Serve with the sambal sauce on the side.

20 whole **dried Thai chiles**

1 pound **dry rice noodles**

10 **shallots**, sliced

1 3-inch knob fresh **turmeric root**, minced, or 2 teaspoons **ground turmeric** plus ½ teaspoon **sugar**

1 2-inch knob **galangal** or fresh **ginger**

4 **lemongrass stalks**, trimmed and thinly sliced

10 **unsalted candlenuts** or **macadamia nuts**

¼ cup **belacan shrimp paste**

8 tablespoons **vegetable oil**

6 cups **shrimp stock** (see page 85) or **chicken broth**

1 15-ounce can **coconut milk**

2 tablespoons **fish sauce**

16 pieces **fried tofu puffs**, each piece cut in half

8 **prawns**, shells and heads on

4 **hard-boiled eggs**, peeled and halved, for serving

1 cup fresh **bean sprouts**

1 medium **cucumber**, peeled and finely julienned, for serving

Fresh **Kaffir lime** or **Vietnamese mint leaves**, thinly sliced, for serving

Spicy Sambal Sauce (page 52), for serving

ISSAN-STYLE PORK

Laab

SERVES 4 TO 6 AS AN APPETIZER, OR 8 TO 10 AS AN HORS D'OEUVRE

Recipes for *laab,* a minced meat dish, vary greatly from region to region all across Thailand. I've highlighted a style characteristic of Issan, a northeastern region where the people are primarily ethnic Lao and Khmer and cook with a lot of heat and funk. Their version of this chopped meat salad includes lime juice and toasted rice powder. The traditional manner of making *laab* requires mincing the meats and grinding the herbs and spices by hand—quite a workout!—but cheating with preground meats and a food processor is perfectly okay. I like to serve my *laab* in cucumber "cups" (a refreshing antidote, along with some sticky rice, to the spiciness of the salad), which makes for beautiful hors d'oeuvres.

In a small bowl, melt the brown sugar in 2 teaspoons of hot water. Add 2 tablespoons of the lime juice and the fish sauce, and stir together. Set aside.

Using a mortar and pestle or a food processor, grind the garlic, fresh chiles, chile flakes, lemongrass, Kaffir lime leaves, coriander, and cardamom into a paste.

Heat the vegetable oil in a wok over medium-high heat, add the paste, and cook for 30 seconds. Raise the heat to high and add the pork and shallots. Cook, breaking up the pork, until the meat is no longer pink, 4 to 5 minutes. Stir in the small bowl of fish sauce with the lime juice and the scallions.

Remove the wok from the heat. Stir in the rice powder, remaining lime juice, red onion, mint, cilantro, and basil.

Serve with the cucumber slices and sticky rice.

2 tablespoons **light brown sugar**

Juice of 2 **limes** (about ½ cup)

2 tablespoons **fish sauce**

8 to 10 large **garlic cloves**, minced

2 fresh **red Thai chiles**, seeded and minced

1 tablespoon crushed **red chile flakes**

1 **lemongrass stalk**, trimmed and finely chopped

2 fresh **Kaffir lime leaves**, thinly sliced

1 teaspoon ground **coriander**

¼ teaspoon ground **cardamom**

2 tablespoons **vegetable oil**

1 pound **ground pork**

4 **shallots**, chopped

2 **scallions** (green and white parts), chopped

2 tablespoons **toasted rice powder** (see Note)

1 small **red onion**, chopped

1 cup fresh **mint leaves**, coarsely torn

1 cup fresh **cilantro leaves**, coarsely torn

1 cup fresh **Thai basil leaves**, coarsely torn

4 large **cucumbers**, sliced, for serving

Cooked warm **Thai sticky rice**, for serving

NOTE

To make your own rice powder, toast
½ cup uncooked sticky rice in a skillet
over low heat, stirring until golden.
Then grind the rice in a spice grinder
or mini processor or pound it with
a mortar and pestle until you have a
fine powder.

NOTE

Even at your local Asian grocery, you're not guaranteed to find betel leaves, which are wild pepper leaves. But other peppery greens like collards or kale are excellent substitutes—just cut them down to 3-inch squares.

FESTIVE THAI LEAF WRAPS

Miang Kham

MAKES 20 TO 30 SMALL BITES, ENOUGH FOR A PARTY OF 6 TO 8

A beautifully wrapped Thai snack bursting with savory-sweet-sour-spicy flavors, *miang kham* embodies much of what I love about the spirit of Thai food, which often transforms humble ingredients into magical feasts. If this recipe, adapted from Chef Jet Ti La, sounds like a lot of ingredients to pack into a little snack, that is in fact what this is—*miang kham* literally means "eating many things in one bite." You can just as easily find *miang kham* sold by roadside vendors in little plastic bags as you can see it ceremoniously plated at Thai temple festivals.

PREPARE THE FILLINGS: Preheat the oven to 350°F. Spread the grated coconut on a baking sheet and bake for 7 to 8 minutes, or until golden brown. Transfer the toasted coconut to a small bowl.

On a large serving platter, arrange the toasted coconut, shallots, lime, ginger, dried shrimp, peanuts, and Thai chiles in individual small bowls. Set aside.

MAKE THE SAUCE: Combine the Thai shrimp paste, galangal, shallots, grated coconut, dried shrimp, ginger, fish sauce, and a couple tablespoons of water in a food processor, and process until you have a thick, smooth paste.

Heat the oil in a medium skillet set over medium heat. Cook the paste until fragrant, 1 to 2 minutes. Add the sugar and 1½ cups of water, and stir to combine. Let the mixture come to a simmer and then cook until it becomes a thick sauce, 10 to 20 minutes.

SERVE THE WRAPS: Have guests fill a betel leaf with their choice of toppings from the platter and top with a little sauce.

FOR THE FILLINGS:

1 cup grated **unsweetened coconut**

½ cup finely diced **shallots**

2 whole **limes**, finely diced with their peel

½ cup finely diced fresh **ginger**

½ cup **dried shrimp**, finely diced

½ cup **unsalted roasted peanuts**

3 to 5 fresh red **Thai chiles**, seeded and finely diced

FOR THE SAUCE:

1 tablespoon **Thai shrimp paste**

½ tablespoon chopped fresh **galangal**

½ tablespoon chopped **shallots**

2 tablespoons grated **unsweetened coconut**

3 tablespoons **dried shrimp**, chopped

1 teaspoon grated fresh **ginger**

2 tablespoons **fish sauce**

1 tablespoon **peanut oil**

2 cups **palm sugar**

20 to 30 fresh **betel nut leaves** (see Note)

JAPANESE PANCAKES

Okonomiyaki

MAKES 2 LARGE PANCAKES, SERVES 4

This savory Japanese pancake varies from home to home, or shop to shop, and meal to meal. This is not surprising, since the dish was originally developed to make use of leftovers. *Okonomi* means "what you like" and *yaki* means "grilled," so *okonomiyaki* is—naturally—"grilled as you like it." Call them latkes or fritters, these cabbage pancakes—which have proliferated around the United States as the *izakaya* trend has grown (see page 58 for more on that)—allow the diner to choose whatever meat or seafood they want incorporated into the batter. At *okonomiyaki* establishments, the server will usually let you inspect the ingredients you've chosen before they are scrambled and poured onto the griddle, often right in front of you.

Mix the ketchup, soy sauce, and Worcestershire in a small bowl and set aside. In a large bowl, whisk together the flour, kosher salt, and baking powder. Beat in 1 cup of cold water and the eggs to make a thick batter. Stir in the cabbage and scallions.

In a large nonstick skillet, heat 1 tablespoon of the vegetable oil and 1 teaspoon of the sesame oil over medium-high heat. Pour in half of the batter and cook for 4 to 5 minutes, lowering the heat slightly if necessary to prevent burning. Arrange 6 bacon pieces on top of the pancake, pressing them down slightly into the batter. Flip the pancake over and continue to cook for 5 to 6 minutes more, until the bacon is crisp and the pancake is golden brown. Transfer the finished pancake to a plate, and repeat with the remaining oils, batter, and bacon.

On a serving plate, drizzle the ketchup mixture over the pancakes. To complete the dish, add squiggles of the mayonnaise on top and garnish with additional scallions.

3 tablespoons **ketchup**

1 teaspoon **soy sauce**

1 teaspoon **Worcestershire sauce**

2 cups **cake flour** or **all-purpose flour** (see Note)

1 teaspoon **kosher salt**

½ teaspoon **baking powder**

4 large **eggs**

4 cups finely **shredded cabbage**

1 bunch **scallions** (white and green parts), thinly sliced, plus more for garnish

2 tablespoons **vegetable oil**

2 teaspoons **Asian sesame oil**

6 slices thin-cut **bacon**, halved crosswise

Japanese Kewpie Mayonnaise, for serving

NOTE

Cake flour closely resembles finely milled Japanese flour, but you can also use all-purpose flour.

CHINESE-MUSLIM LAMB BURGERS

Rou Jia Mo

SERVES 5 TO 6

Think of *rou jia mo* as the Chinese equivalent of a hamburger—one that features the distinctive flavors of the street foods favored by one of China's oldest ethnic and religious minorities. In the Muslim quarters of Beijing, and in other Muslim-concentrated parts of China such as Xi'an, much of China's multicultural heritage dating back to the Silk Road era is preserved. As the original capital city of China, Xi'an is a melting pot of many religions, ideas, and cuisines. The food is roughly referred to as "Chinese Muslim" and features Middle Eastern staples such as flatbreads and lamb (as opposed to Chinese staples of rice and pork), as well as lots of flavorings that traveled the 4,000 miles of the Silk Road: cumin, scallions, onions, and chiles. (I imagine that this is something that Marco Polo would have eaten.) Since many Muslims do not eat pork, there are a number of halal butcher shops and restaurants, where still today you can easily follow your nose to the likes of lamb skewers and these tasty burgers.

PREPARE THE LAMB: Heat the oil in a large stockpot over medium-high heat. Add the lamb pieces and cook for 4 to 5 minutes, until lightly browned. Add the garlic, ginger, peppercorns, cumin, salt, black pepper, and red chile flakes. Cook, stirring, for 1 minute, until the spices are fragrant. Add 3 cups of water and the soy sauce, bring to a boil, and then reduce the heat to medium-low. Simmer gently for 1½ hours, or until the lamb is very tender, adding a little more water as needed so the meat is saucy, not dry.

recipe continues

FOR THE LAMB:

1 tablespoon **vegetable oil**

1 pound **lean lamb** (such as leg meat, stew meat, or deboned shoulder chops), cubed

3 **garlic cloves**, minced

1 1-inch knob fresh **ginger**, minced

1 teaspoon **Sichuanese peppercorns**, lightly crushed

1 teaspoon ground **cumin**

1 teaspoon **kosher salt**

1 teaspoon freshly **ground black pepper**

½ teaspoon crushed **red chile flakes**

¼ cup **soy sauce**

FOR THE BUNS:

1 teaspoon **active dry yeast**

½ teaspoon **sugar**

3 cups **all-purpose flour**, plus more for shaping the buns

1 teaspoon **kosher salt**

Fresh **cilantro leaves**, for serving

Chopped **scallions** (white and green parts), for serving

MAKE THE BUN DOUGH: Pour 1½ cups of warm water into a small bowl, and stir in the yeast and sugar. Allow to sit for about 10 minutes, until the yeast blooms. In a large bowl, stir together the flour and kosher salt. Make a well in the center of the flour and add the yeast mixture, stirring just enough to make a smooth dough (no need to knead it further). Cover the bowl with plastic wrap and set it aside in a warm place for 1 hour, or until the dough has nearly doubled in volume.

When the lamb is very tender, use a slotted spoon to lift it onto a cutting board. Coarsely chop the meat and return it to the sauce.

Preheat the oven to 350°F. Heat a dry cast-iron skillet over medium heat.

SHAPE THE BUNS: Dust your hands and a clean work surface with flour. Scoop out a lump of dough about the size of a clementine orange and flatten it on the floured surface. Using your hands, stretch the dough out to form a rope about 10 inches long. Flatten the rope with your palms, then roll the dough up on itself from one end to the other, creating a tight spiral. Set the dough spiral up and flatten it with your palm into a disk about 4 inches wide. (The rolling and flattening gives the finished bun its characteristic chewy layers.) Repeat with the remaining dough to make 10 to 12 buns.

Place 3 buns in the heated dry skillet and cook for 2 to 3 minutes, until the underside is lightly browned. Flip and cook for 2 to 3 minutes to brown the second side. Place the browned buns on an ungreased baking sheet, and repeat with the remaining buns. Bake the buns for 10 minutes, until they start to crisp.

SERVE THE BURGERS: Slit the warm buns in half horizontally, like a pita pocket, and fill them with the lamb. Top with the cilantro leaves and scallions. Spoon on some of the sauce from the lamb, and serve at once.

TIP

The traditional buns for this dish aren't readily available at grocery stores. You can either make your own with this recipe or substitute warm pita bread.

FOOD AS MEMORY: A CRAVING FOR BEEF NOODLE SOUP

I return to Taiwan as often as I can, and each time I reunite with my near-century-old grandmother at her dining table. In the family portraits hanging on her walls, I am a preteen with braces, and she—front and center—is the proud matriarch, unabashedly draped with showy jewelry and sporting dragon-lady-red lipstick. After a lifetime of nonstop work, her body and mind are weathered, and there's not much for her to do now except eat, sleep, and, of course, play mahjong. But she has left a legacy not just for our family, but really for all of Taiwan.

When the Communists took over China, my grandma fled with her family from Zhejiang province to the nearby island of Taiwan. They lost everything in the process— beloved relatives, property, belongings, and, along the way, my grandfather's will to start over again. The only thing left, seemingly, was my grandmother's tenacity. She fed her family with her earnings from washing and mending other people's clothes, and she eventually bought real estate on the outskirts of Taipei. When my grandfather died, she moved to Saudi Arabia to develop real estate. Just imagine: an uneducated woman in her fifties who spoke only Chinese, moving to the desert and to a culture where women's faces were shrouded by veils, and ending up as the boss. As far as grandmotherly wisdom goes, her advice to me was that "the key to success in life is to be half-woman/half-man."

Her appetite for food, as for life, was outsize. We used to marvel at the number of dumplings she could eat in a sitting—a dozen or even two dozen wasn't enough. But when it comes to eating these days, she couldn't be grumpier. She objects to most food like a baby being cajoled to eat pureed peas and turns away from succulent fresh steamed fish and other delicacies.

Remarkably, there is one dish that she still hungers for: Taiwanese beef noodle soup. My grandmother has slurped down literally hundreds of bowls over the decades, and this is one of the few dishes that she still eats with gusto. Food—and flavor—has an astonishingly rejuvenating effect on memory. When my grandmother eats the soup, it's as though she is young again, in charge of her appetite and her fate. Food is memory—it nourishes us even when we're too old to remember our taste for it.

TAIWANESE BEEF NOODLE SOUP

Niu Ro Mian

SERVES 6 TO 8

If there is a national dish for Taiwan, it is beef noodle soup, which is found everywhere from night markets to traditional dining halls. At beef noodle soup shops, the vendors tend to their enormous cauldrons with great affection, as if raising a child. These are master soups that are never emptied, but only added to—more bones, more onions—to build on yesterday's flavors. I love the idea of a broth that intensifies over time, the way a wok benefits from being properly seasoned over time and through use.

This Taiwanese version of the classic Chinese beef noodle soup is "red-braised" (slow-cooked in soy sauce). The recipe is adapted from my grandmother's favorite: the soup served at Taipei's Yong Kang Jie Beef Noodles—a hole-in-the-wall joint that is now a "must" destination on every foodie's list of where to eat in Taipei.

In a large pot, heat one tablespoon of the oil over moderate heat. Add the beef shank and tendons and cook until browned all over, about 15 minutes. Transfer the beef to a bowl and set aside.

In the same pot, heat the remaining tablespoon of oil. Add the ginger, garlic, onion, and chiles and cook until fragrant, about 2 minutes. Add the sugar and tomatoes and continue to cook until the sugar has dissolved and the tomatoes have softened, about 5 minutes. Add the chili bean paste and continue to cook for an additional minute.

recipe continues

2 tablespoons **vegetable oil**

2 pounds **beef shank**, cut into 4 large pieces

1 pound **beef tendons**

6 large slices fresh **ginger**

9 **garlic cloves**, crushed

1 large **yellow onion**, chopped

3 small fresh **red Thai chiles**, seeded and chopped

2 tablespoons **sugar**

4 medium **Roma tomatoes**, sliced

2 tablespoons **chili bean paste** (*doubanjiang*)

1 cup **Shaoxing rice wine**

4 **star anise pods**

1 tablespoon crushed **Sichuanese peppercorns**

1 cup **soy sauce**, plus more to taste

½ pound **leafy greens**, such as baby bok choy or spinach

Black vinegar, to taste

2 pounds **Asian wheat noodles**

Preserved mustard greens (see page 40), chopped, for serving

Fresh **cilantro** (leaves and stems), coarsely chopped, for serving

Scallions (light green and white parts), chopped, for serving

Return the browned meat and tendons to the pot. Add the Shaoxing wine, scraping up the browned bits from the bottom of the pot. Add the star anise, crushed peppercorns, soy sauce, and about 2 quarts of water. Bring the liquid to a boil; then lower the heat to a simmer. Cover the pot and cook, occasionally skimming any fat and debris off the surface, until the meat is meltingly tender, about 2 hours or longer for the tendons.

Transfer the beef shanks and tendons to a cutting board. Strain the soup through a colander into a clean pot, and discard the solids. When the beef and tendons have cooled, chop both into 1-inch slivers and add the meat to the strained broth. Bring the broth back to a slight boil, add the greens, and simmer just until tender. Season the soup with black vinegar and additional soy sauce to taste.

Cook the noodles in a large pot of boiling water according to the package directions, and drain them. Divide the noodles among large soup bowls, and pour the soup over them. Serve the mustard greens, cilantro, and scallions on the side, so each diner can pile them on in whatever order and amount they like.

★ ★ TIP

My kids are fans of pho, the Vietnamese beef noodle soup, so I'll sometimes adapt this recipe by using broad rice noodles instead of the wheat noodles. Both beef-based soups are slow-simmered, are flavored with aromatics like star anise and peppercorns, and are hearty and belly-warming.

FUNKY FOODS

SAMBAL STINGRAY
Page 51

Why do funky foods taste so damn good? Some of my favorite Asian foods—kimchi, fish sauce, miso—smell stinky and yet are awfully appetizing. That fermented funk is popular across many cultures: sourdough breads, yogurt, sauerkraut, and beer are just a few famous foods that harness the transformative "culture of culture." But with Asian food in particular, funk is a defining flavor characteristic. Because we taste food first through our noses, these foods set off our olfactory sensors.

Most of us also have certain food flavors that we find personally offensive. I used to be terrified of kimchi, the pungent, bright red Korean delicacy that my dad kept in a jar tucked away in the back of the fridge. To me it smelled like dirty feet or an old rag—and besides, what could possibly taste good that was made from cabbage? But now I'm slightly obsessed with kimchi, which has also expanded my palate for other funky flavors. I eat it as a spicy condiment to kick up my Korean barbecue or simply with rice and fried eggs.

Just as other centuries-old fermented food projects like beer and pickle-making have cultivated new, young devotees, kimchi is enjoying a renaissance—even though its flavors have, for the most part, stayed the same. It's our collective palate that has evolved to crave more of the foreign flavors like fermented fish sauce that we experience on our travels.

I'm fascinated by the love of fermented foods across cultures: the French and Italians treat rotten, aged milk made into cheese as a national treasure, and I'm sure the stench of Taiwan's *chòu dòufu* (stinky tofu) doesn't smell like roses to most foreigners. Yet Parmesan, stinky tofu, and kimchi are all sources of cultural pride and carry with them an esteemed history that has been carried down through generations. In acquiring an appreciation for fermented foods from foreign cultures, we also add to our own cultural heritage.

GARLICKY SMASHED CUCUMBER PICKLES

Tsukemono

MAKES 2 CUPS

Pickles are everyday food in much of Asian cuisine—especially in Japan, where nary a meal goes by without them. This dish comes together in minutes once the cucumbers are briefly bathed in a brine of salt, vinegar, and garlic (but of course they can be pickled for longer to intensify the flavors). I love how fresh and raw this simple dish tastes, thanks especially to the huge dose of garlic. The longer you brine the pickles, the more they will soften, but the heat of the garlic will also intensify. This is a dish you can snack on or pair with practically anything—either as a tangy counterpart to a richer meal or as a spicy, salty pickle to add flavor to a bowl of rice.

8 **Persian or Japanese cucumbers**, unpeeled, cut in half lengthwise, then diagonally into 1-inch chunks
1 teaspoon **salt**
8 **garlic cloves**, smashed
2 tablespoons **mirin**
2 tablespoons **rice vinegar**
2 tablespoons **light soy sauce**
1 tablespoon **sugar**
2 tablespoons **Asian sesame oil**

Place the cucumber pieces on a cutting board. Smash them lightly using the side of a broad knife blade, such as a Chinese cleaver. Place the smashed cucumbers in a bowl and sprinkle with the salt. Let stand for 15 to 30 minutes; then drain off the accumulated liquid.

Add the garlic, mirin, rice vinegar, soy sauce, sugar, and sesame oil to the cucumbers, and stir to combine. Cover the bowl with plastic wrap and let the mixture mellow in the refrigerator for at least 15 minutes and up to an hour. Served chilled.

★ ★ NOTE Although most pickles are brined for longer periods of time in order to produce a sour-tasting lactic acid, a quick soak is all you need to make this fresh dish.

TOFU WITH THOUSAND-YEAR EGGS

SERVES 4 AS A SIDE DISH

The name of this dish makes it sound much more sensational than it really is; however, what's bizarre to one culture may simply be everyday grub to another, as thousand-year eggs are to the Chinese. Rather than a millennium, these eggs are preserved for a few weeks in a mixture of clay, ash, salt, quicklime, and rice hull. This process transforms the duck eggs so that the yolk turns a dark greenish-gray color with a pronounced creaminess and the smell of sulphur and ammonia, while the white becomes translucent, darkened, and jelly-like. This assembled dish requires no actual cooking, but it carries extraordinary flavor and is a great complement to Turkey Congee (page 155).

1 pound **soft ("silken") tofu**

2 **preserved duck eggs** (also called **"century eggs"**), peeled and quartered

2 tablespoons **soy sauce**

2 tablespoons **Asian sesame oil**

2 tablespoons coarsely chopped fresh **cilantro** (leaves and stems)

2 **scallions** (green and white parts), thinly sliced

Cube the tofu by slicing it in half horizontally; then slice it lengthwise once and crosswise twice so that you end up with 12 pieces. Arrange the tofu slices on a serving plate, and top with the quartered duck eggs. Just before serving, drizzle with the soy sauce and sesame oil, and scatter the cilantro and scallions over the top.

FAVA BEAN PUREE WITH PRESERVED MUSTARD GREENS

SERVES 6 TO 8 AS AN APPETIZER

Dishes made with fava beans (or broad beans) are popular in Shanghainese restaurants, served as a part of other assorted small bites before a meal. Fresh fava beans make regular appearances at local greenmarkets in the Bay Area, and whenever I see them, I grab several pounds for my grandmother, who immigrated decades ago but still thinks of fava beans affectionately as a Shanghainese vegetable. Though it is a lot of work, she shells and peels each bean by hand, so that an entire bagful yields only a handful of tender beans—which she nimbly transforms into this nostalgic recipe from her childhood that she has passed on to me.

The preserved mustard greens are easy to make on your own, and they give this fresh vegetal dip a great briny finish. Preserved mustard greens can be purchased in most Asian groceries in a pinch, but the pickling process is easy, similar to making sauerkraut, and the end result is sweet, salty, and crunchy.

FOR THE PRESERVED MUSTARD GREENS:
1 pound fresh **mustard greens**, tough stems and inedible rough leaves discarded, remainder coarsely chopped
Sea salt, for pickling the greens
1 tablespoon **distilled white vinegar**

MAKE THE PRESERVED MUSTARD GREENS: In a large pickling jar, pack a tight layer of the leaves and sprinkle the leaves liberally with sea salt. Repeat the layers, packing firmly, until the jar is full. Cover the mustard greens with water, and then add the vinegar (to prevent mold) to top off the jar. Cover it tightly, and shake it a couple of times so that the vinegar is evenly distributed throughout the jar.

Let the jar sit, unrefrigerated, for at least 3 days; the amount of time it takes to pickle will vary according to the temperature—anywhere from 3 days in the summer heat to 10 days in the winter cold. The greens are ready when they have turned completely brown. Drain the water from the greens and transfer the greens to their own jar. (You will have about 1 cup preserved greens; they will keep refrigerated for up to a year, like sauerkraut or pickles.)

MAKE THE FAVA BEAN PUREE: Finely chop the preserved mustard greens to yield about ¼ cup. Heat the vegetable oil in a wok over medium-high heat. Once it is sizzling, add the garlic and stir-fry until fragrant, about 30 seconds. Add the chopped preserved greens and sauté for another minute. Add the fava beans and sauté for 2 more minutes, until they start to brown around the edges. Add the chicken broth, cover the wok, and simmer over low heat for 10 to 15 minutes, until the fava beans are tender.

Remove the wok from the heat, and mash the fava beans right in the wok with a potato masher or the back of a spoon until the desired texture is reached. (I prefer a hummus-like texture, but some people like it smoother or chunkier.) Spoon the fava bean puree into a serving dish and drizzle it lightly with sesame oil. Serve with rice crackers if desired.

FOR THE FAVA BEAN PUREE:

2 tablespoons **vegetable oil**

2 **garlic cloves**, finely minced

3 pounds fresh **fava beans**, shelled and peeled (2½ to 3 cups peeled beans)

½ cup **chicken broth** or water

Asian sesame oil, to taste

Rice crackers, for dipping (optional)

MALAYSIAN OKRA WITH SHRIMP PASTE

SERVES 6 AS PART OF A LARGER MEAL

The major flavor component of this dish is *belacan* (fermented shrimp paste), which is perhaps Malaysia's equivalent to Korea's kimchi. My favorite version of this Malaysian staple, fancifully known as "lady fingers," is made with okra, but the dish is also delicious with *kang kung* (water spinach, found in Chinatown markets) or yam leaves (which are now popping up in greenmarkets). Though the fundamentals for Malaysian cuisine are built on Thai, Chinese, and Indian flavors, dishes like this are still relatively unpopular in the United States, perhaps because of their funkiness. No surprise: this fermented shrimp paste becomes very stinky—as in sweaty-socks-stinky—when heated. It's an acquired taste, but one that perfumes the night markets of Malaysia and Singapore—and, now, my kitchen.

3 tablespoons **vegetable oil**

3 **garlic cloves**, chopped

2 tablespoons ***belacan* shrimp paste**

2 tablespoons **Spicy Sambal Sauce** (page 52)

1 pound **okra**, sliced diagonally (see Note)

Fish sauce, to taste

Perfect Steamed Rice (page 145), for serving

Heat a large wok over high heat and swirl in the vegetable oil. Add the garlic and stir-fry until fragrant, about 30 seconds. Add the *belacan* paste and sambal sauce, and fry until the wok is smoky and the pungency of the *belacan* paste is released, about 3 minutes.

Add the okra. Continue to stir quickly until it softens, about 8 minutes. Season with fish sauce, and serve with steamed rice.

★ ★ NOTE

If you dislike the signature goop that comes with fresh okra, you can presoak the sliced vegetable in a quart of water mixed with a cup of cider vinegar for about an hour before draining and cooking (though the added texture helps thicken this dish).

THE KIMCHI RENAISSANCE

The stereotype of Koreans consuming so much kimchi that their pores emanate garlic and chile is true, at least from what I've observed. After all, Korea's per capita kimchi consumption is an astonishing 40 pounds a year! To make kimchi, *gochugaru* (red chile flakes) is mixed with garlic, ginger, and anchovy paste to make the *gochujang* paste, which is then massaged into napa cabbage leaves until the leaves start to go limp from the salt and fiery red from the chiles. Korean wives (or at least the good ones, we are told) know how well seasoned their kimchi is by touch *only*—now *that* is talent. In the olden days, fresh vegetables, especially in the winter, were scarce, and so women were responsible for salting and burying the summer cabbage crop in earthenware pots deep in the ground, to give the family a preserved source of vitamin C to ward off scurvy in the winter months.

Part of the toil of making kimchi is the burn of the heat as the chiles soak into your hands. To me, the tradition of the "kimchi burn" explains so much about Korean culture and its emphasis on the nobility that comes from suffering for your family. It is told that one of the first bonding experiences a Korean wife has with her mother-in-law takes place when the she learns the family's kimchi recipe. Suffering for your art, of course, does have an upside: Korean beauty companies have discovered that women who spend a lifetime making kimchi have baby-soft hands as a result. Who would've thought—anti-aging skin care as a by-product of the fermented cabbage in your fridge!

Beauty benefits aside, my favorite thing about kimchi is that it perks up so many foods. It transforms a boring dish like leftover rice into something to crave and turns surprising pairings—Korean tacos, anyone? (see page 117)—into instant classics. If you want to have an Asian cooking adventure, I can think of no better journey. Just channel your inner Korean grandma.

INSTANT KIMCHI

MAKES ABOUT 1 GALLON

Even though most kimchi is fermented, it is also delicious fresh. This recipe makes a big batch so that you can have some right away and then store the rest to ferment over time. You will need a big plastic basin or maybe a bucket to make it, or even use your sink or bathtub to supersize it. Of course you can also make smaller batches if you like by halving the recipe. The cabbage will wilt dramatically once it's been salted. The Korean chile pepper flakes, *gochugaru*, which I use liberally, are made by drying Korean red chile peppers in the sun, then seeding and crushing them into flakes. The bright red pepper flakes look fiery and intimidating, but they are actually milder than they appear, which is why I use them by the cupful.

Kimchi's character changes over time as it ferments in the refrigerator. This kimchi is delicious eaten right away as a fresh and crunchy side salad that's perfect in Kimchi Tacos (page 117) or with rice and sunny-side-up fried eggs as a simple lunch. As the kimchi ferments, it will continue to sour and wilt, becoming more suitable for use in stews like Seafood *Soondubu* with Kimchi (page 48).

Place the sliced cabbage in a large bowl and add water to cover. Add the salt, stir to combine, and soak for 1 hour, stirring every 15 minutes, until the cabbage starts to wilt.

Meanwhile, bring 2 cups of water to a boil in a small saucepan, and stir in the glutinous rice flour until well combined. Stir in the sugar, and simmer until the mixture forms a thick porridge. Set aside to cool.

To make the *gochujang* chili paste, pour the glutinous rice mixture into a large bowl. Add the fish sauce, garlic, ginger, and *gochugaru* flakes and mix together. Set aside.

recipe continues

1 large head **napa cabbage** (about 3½ pounds), quartered lengthwise and then sliced into 1½-inch-wide pieces

1 cup **kosher salt**

½ cup **sweet glutinous rice flour**

½ cup **sugar**

¼ cup **fish sauce**

10 **garlic cloves**, smashed and coarsely chopped

1 1-inch knob fresh **ginger**, minced

1 cup *gochugaru* **flakes**

1 large **daikon**, quartered and thinly sliced

1 medium **carrot**, quartered and thinly sliced

½ **yellow onion**, diced

1 bunch **scallions** (green and white parts), chopped

2 **leeks** (white parts only), thinly sliced

½ cup **dried anchovies** or **dried baby shrimp** (optional)

2 tablespoons **sesame seeds**

Drain the salted cabbage, rinse it under cool running water, and then squeeze out any excess water. In a very large container, combine the drained cabbage with the daikon, carrot, onion, scallions, and leeks. If you want a stronger umami flavor in the kimchi, stir the dried anchovies or shrimp into the cabbage. Stir in the *gochujang* to coat the vegetables completely. Sprinkle the sesame seeds on top to serve.

Pack the leftover kimchi into several large jars, leaving a little room on the top for some natural bubbling as the fermentation process takes place.

SEAFOOD *SOONDUBU* WITH KIMCHI

SERVES 4

Soondubu makes a hearty family stew that will leave your house smelling of kimchi (a good thing, of course) for days to come. Like many Korean stews, this dish is traditionally served table-side, so for a little extra flair, I recommend setting up a butane burner beneath the stew in a traditional Asian clay pot, so your guests can dig in (or if you don't have a clay pot, you can also set a Dutch oven over a butane burner or bring the pot to the table). Either way, the stew should be served bubbling, spooned over rice. One pot will provide a hearty meal for four, but you can always stretch it as part of a kimchi-themed spread with some LA Galbi short ribs (see page 132) and Kimchi Pancakes (opposite).

Heat the vegetable oil in a deep soup pot or a clay pot set over medium heat. Add the onion and cook until softened, about 2 minutes. Mix in the *gochujang* to coat. Add the kimchi, broth, and soy sauce and bring to a simmer. Season with sea salt to taste. Add the zucchini and simmer for about 2 minutes, until soft. Add the tofu in big loose spoonfuls, like scooping up ice cream. Simmer the tofu gently for 3 to 4 minutes, until heated through. Throw in the oysters and clams, cover, and simmer for 3 to 4 minutes, until the clams just open. Remove and discard any unopened clams.

Crack the eggs directly into the simmering liquid. Let the eggs cook for 1 to 2 minutes (the runny yolks will add a silky complexity to the dish).

Garnish with the scallions, and serve immediately with hot rice.

2 tablespoons **vegetable oil**

1 medium **onion**, diced

2 to 4 tablespoons ***gochujang* chili paste**, homemade (see page 45) or store-bought, to taste

1 cup **Instant Kimchi** (page 45) or store-bought kimchi

2 cups **chicken broth**

1 tablespoon **soy sauce**

Sea salt, to taste

1 medium **zucchini**, cut into ¼-inch cubes

1 pound **soft ("silken") tofu**, drained

1 cup freshly **shucked oysters**, or 1 8-ounce can shucked oysters

12 **littleneck clams**, cleaned and debearded

4 large **eggs**

2 **scallions** (green and white parts), thinly sliced lengthwise

Perfect Steamed Rice (page 145), for serving

KIMCHI PANCAKES

SERVES 6

For a variation on Chinese scallion pancakes, this is a good one to expand your repertoire. I make two large pancakes with the ingredients here, but you can make smaller individual ones if you prefer. At Korean restaurants, you will typically receive small dishes of *banchan* (meaning "side dishes") that are set in the middle of the table for everyone to share. These pancakes might be served as a *banchan* along with a main dish like Grilled Korean Short Ribs (page 132) or a pot of soupy stew like Seafood *Soondubu* with Kimchi (opposite), or both! A more luxurious version of this pancake can be made with the addition of seafood—simply substitute 1 cup chopped raw seafood for 1 cup of the kimchi (squid and shrimp are good quick-cooking choices).

MAKE THE DIPPING SAUCE: In a small bowl, stir together the soy sauce, black vinegar, kimchi brine, and sesame oil. Set aside.

MAKE THE PANCAKES: In a large bowl, combine the flour and sea salt; then add 1 cup of water and stir until mixed well. Add the kimchi, brine, and sliced scallions and combine until mixed.

Heat 2 tablespoons of the vegetable oil in a large skillet. Spoon half of the pancake batter into the skillet and spread it out evenly to form a round. Cook for about 2 minutes, until the bottom is browned and crispy. Flip the pancake over and cook the other side for about 2 minutes. (If you have added seafood to the batter, double the cooking time for each side.) Transfer the finished pancake to a paper towel–lined plate, and repeat with the remaining oil and batter.

Cut the pancakes into bite-size pieces to serve, and garnish with sesame seeds and chopped scallions if desired. Serve with the dipping sauce on the side.

FOR THE DIPPING SAUCE:

¼ cup **soy sauce**

3 tablespoons **black vinegar**

3 tablespoons **kimchi brine** (see page 45)

3 tablespoons **Asian sesame oil**

FOR THE PANCAKES:

1½ cups **all-purpose flour**

1 teaspoon **fine sea salt**

1½ cups chopped **Instant Kimchi** (page 45) or store-bought kimchi, plus 6 tablespoons of its brine

8 **scallions** (green and white parts), sliced diagonally into 1-inch pieces

4 tablespoons **vegetable oil**

1 tablespoon **toasted sesame seeds**, for garnish (optional)

Chopped **scallions** (green and white parts), for garnish (optional)

SAMBAL STINGRAY

SERVES 4

The first time I had this dish was at a joint in Singapore's red-light district—the type of place with just plastic stools for seats, swarming mosquitos, outdoor bathrooms, and prostitutes lurking on the dark street corners, a perfect backdrop to fuel a tourist's image of the seedier side of Singaporean street food culture. The stingray that we found there, with its toasted sambal and *belacan* sauce, stunk in the most appetizing way possible. Where stingray is not available, substitute its cousin, skate, whose wings taste and look very similar.

In its simplest form, sambal is just chile peppers and salt, the Southeast Asian equivalent of ketchup, but my version also contains shrimp paste to add to the funk. Though sambals can easily be made in a food processor, I prefer to make mine the traditional way with a mortar and pestle, which creates a coarser and more homemade texture. Sambal will keep in the refrigerator for about a month.

2 tablespoons **vegetable oil**

2 fresh **banana leaves**, rinsed and patted dry

½ cup **Spicy Sambal Sauce** (recipe follows)

1½ pounds **stingray or skate wing fillets** (ask your fishmonger to bone and fillet the spiky fish)

Perfect Steamed Rice (page 145), for serving

Set a large dry skillet on high heat to preheat for 5 minutes. Then pour in the vegetable oil and swirl it to coat the pan. Lay a banana leaf in the pan. Spread half of the sambal sauce evenly over the fish and lay the fish, sambal side down, on the banana leaf. Cover the pan tightly, reduce the heat to medium, and cook for 5 minutes.

Remove the fish and the banana leaf from the pan, and place a fresh banana leaf in the pan. Spread the remaining sambal sauce over the fish and flip the fish onto the fresh banana leaf in the pan (with the uncooked side down). Cover the fish with the cooked banana leaf, then cover the pan with a lid. Cook over medium heat for 5 minutes or so, until the fish is cooked and the sambal and banana leaves are fragrant.

Serve with hot steamed rice.

recipe continues

SPICY SAMBAL SAUCE

MAKES ABOUT 2 CUPS

Bring 2 cups of water to a boil in a medium saucepan.

Heat a dry wok over high heat for 3 minutes, and then add the dried chiles. Toss or stir for 30 seconds to 1 minute, until they start to lighten slightly in color. Add the toasted chiles to the saucepan of boiling water, remove from heat, and soak for 20 minutes.

Using a mortar and pestle, grind the ginger, garlic, and lemongrass together until coarsely ground. Drain the soaked chiles and add the fresh and drained chiles to the mortar; continue to pound to make a coarse paste. Add the rice vinegar and salt and continue pounding. At this point you should have a smooth but fairly liquid slurry.

In a medium saucepan, heat the sambal slurry until it is just simmering. Stir in the sugar and *belacan* and continue cooking, stirring frequently, until the sugar has dissolved and the mixture has thickened slightly, about 10 minutes. The prepared sambal will keep in the refrigerator for about 1 month.

¼ pound dried **red serrano chiles**, stemmed, coarsely chopped, seeds discarded

1 2-inch knob fresh **ginger**, chopped

1 head **garlic** (about 20 cloves), chopped

1 **lemongrass stalk** (pale green and white parts), trimmed and chopped

10 fresh **red Thai chiles**, seeded

1 cup **rice vinegar**

2 teaspoons **salt**

2 teaspoons **sugar**

¼ cup **belacan shrimp paste**

FILIPINO CHICKEN ADOBO

SERVES 6

Funky chicken adobo, a falling-apart stew made with fermented fish sauce and vinegar, is found everywhere in the Philippines, but no two households make this hallmark dish in quite the same way. This isn't surprising when you consider that the Philippines is a large archipelago made up of more than 7,000 islands, each with its own regional flavors. On top of that, Filipino culture truly represents a cultural crossroads, with a blended population of Malays, Hindus, Arabs, Chinese, Spaniards, and Americans. In the United States, Filipinos are the second-largest Asian American demographic (after the Chinese), yet their cuisine has until recently been relatively under-the-radar outside of their own community. Happily, that is changing, thanks to a new generation of young, proud Filipino Americans who are spreading their cuisine from Manhattan's Lower East Side to the San Gabriel Valley.

3 pounds bone-in, skin-on **chicken thighs**

1 15-ounce can diced **tomatoes**, drained

1 cup **distilled white vinegar**

¼ cup **soy sauce**

2 tablespoons **fish sauce**

10 **garlic cloves**, chopped

2 tablespoons freshly **ground black pepper**

2 **bay leaves**

2 tablespoons **olive oil**

2 medium **onions**, sliced

2 **scallions** (green and white parts), sliced

Perfect Steamed Rice (page 145), for serving

In a large bowl, add the chicken, tomatoes, vinegar, soy sauce, fish sauce, garlic, black pepper, and bay leaves. Cover and refrigerate overnight.

Place the chicken and its marinade in a large, heavy pot and set it over medium-high heat. Bring to a boil, reduce the heat to medium, and simmer uncovered for 30 to 35 minutes, until the chicken is cooked through. Transfer the chicken to a plate. Set aside. Skim off any fat from the surface of the sauce. Bring the sauce to a boil, and cook until it has reduced by half, 8 to 10 minutes.

In a large skillet, heat the olive oil over medium-high heat. Add the chicken, skin side down, and sear until the skin browns, 6 to 8 minutes. Flip the chicken, and add the onions to the pan. Cook until the chicken is browned and the onions are lightly colored, 8 to 10 minutes. Toss sauce with the chicken and onions. Serve over rice with scallions.

VIETNAMESE LEMONGRASS CHICKEN WITH FISH SAUCE

SERVES 6

If there's one dish that's landing with regularity on busy weeknight dinner tables from coast to coast, it's roast chicken. This Vietnamese version can sit overnight or up to 24 hours in a marinade of fermented fish sauce and lemongrass and is ready to pop into the oven as soon as you get home from work. In Vietnam, lemongrass is typically used as an aromatic and is simmered in soups and stews, but this recipe calls for finely chopping the lemongrass to bring out its incredible fragrance and to add texture to the chicken. I like to arrange seasonal vegetables (like quartered artichokes and carrots in the spring, and parsnips and Jerusalem artichokes in the fall) underneath the chicken in the pan so they can soak up the caramelized juices while roasting.

2 to 3 **lemongrass stalks**, trimmed and finely chopped (about ¾ cup chopped)

4 medium **shallots**, chopped

¼ cup **fish sauce**

1 teaspoon **sea salt**

2 tablespoons **sugar**

1 whole **chicken** (3½ to 4 pounds)

1 pound **assorted seasonal vegetables** (see headnote)

In a small bowl, combine the lemongrass, shallots, fish sauce, sea salt, and sugar. Place the chicken in a large dish. Spread the lemongrass marinade evenly over the chicken, tucking any excess into its cavity. Cover and refrigerate overnight. When you are ready to cook it, bring the chicken to room temperature.

Preheat the oven to 350°F. Scatter the vegetables in a large roasting pan or cast-iron skillet. Place the chicken, breast side down, on top of the vegetables. Roast the chicken for 30 minutes. Then turn the chicken over so it is breast side up and spoon the pan juices over the top. Roast for 1 hour, until the thickest part of the thigh registers 180°F on an instant-read thermometer. (If the skin starts to char, cover the chicken with aluminum foil. You can also add a little water to the pan if the pan juices start to burn.) Remove the chicken and let it cool slightly before carving. Serve with the vegetables on the side.

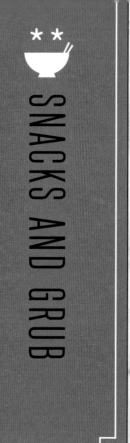

SNACKS AND GRUB

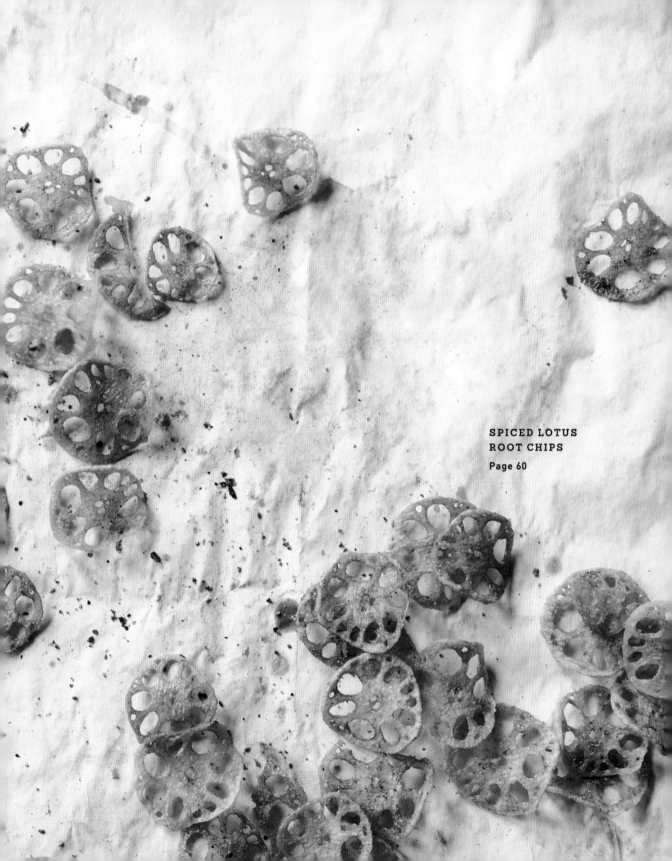

SPICED LOTUS
ROOT CHIPS
Page 60

In food-obsessed cities like Taipei and Tokyo, there is always something to whet your appetite—tea eggs by convenience store cash registers and even vending machines that sell ramen and sake to fortify weary commuters on train station platforms. It's fast food, Asian-style, and it's so much more than a hot dog from a cart. In Asia's fastest-moving metropolises like Tokyo, Hong Kong, and Shanghai, eating between meals is a way of life. Luckily eating on the go need not come at the expense of good food.

My favorite places to visit whenever I'm in Asia are the food courts, which are located in the basement of most department stores. These are epicurean meccas, where a collection of vendors will entice you with tapioca tea, bento boxes, and Japanese confectionary like *dango* (page 146). See if you can walk out of one of these empty-handed. I never can!

During midday meetings at the office, tea and snacks are frequently served: often a mixture of preserved fruit, seeds, and nuts; or perhaps watermelon seeds and umami-packed dried squid. Train stations are not only transportation hubs but also food centers where you can pop into a spinning-sushi-bar restaurant, find a perch at the bar, and enjoy small "boats" of freshly made sushi as they rotate on the conveyor belt in front of you. At a *ramen-ya*, don't be surprised if there are no seats; it's customary for customers to slurp standing up. In fact, the average amount of time that is spent at a *ramen-ya* is an efficient 13 minutes!

After the sun sets, there is the *izakaya* scene, Japanese-style gastropubs where small bites such as grilled sardines (see page 67), fried chicken *karaage* (see page 65), and Spiced Lotus Root Chips (page 60) are brought out as the kitchen prepares them, and beer and *shochu*, a distilled Asian spirit, are served into the early morning hours.

Asian cities don't stop, and fuel is never far from reach so that you, too, can operate 24/7. From day into night—at the morning's open-air markets, between commutes at train stations, or after work at night markets—the food is ready whenever you are.

FIERY EDAMAME WITH GARLIC MISO

SERVES 4

A popular starter at Japanese restaurants, edamame (immature soybeans in the pod) are also a great snack and drinking companion. In the United States, edamame can be found fresh at greenmarkets in the fall, but they are also available frozen year-round. In this recipe, the beans are tossed in a spicy miso sauce, which adds complexity to the naturally sweet and briny flavor of edamame.

Prepare the edamame according to the package instructions, or until just steamed through. Transfer the cooked edamame to a serving bowl.

In a small skillet, heat the vegetable oil over high heat. Add the garlic and chili sauce to the hot oil, and cook until combined and fragrant, 30 seconds. Add the miso and mix together for another minute.

Remove the skillet from the heat and pour the spicy miso mixture over the edamame. Toss to coat, and serve immediately.

1 pound frozen **edamame** in their pods

2 tablespoons **vegetable oil**

4 **garlic cloves**, minced

4 tablespoons **chili sauce**, such as sambal (see page 52)

2 tablespoons **red or white miso paste**

★ ★
NOTE

In lieu of potato chips and other starchy, fatty foods, lots of Asian snacks are made with nutrient-packed beans like edamame, nuts, seeds, dried seaweed, and even dried meats and seafood (dried squid is very popular).

SPICED LOTUS ROOT CHIPS

MAKES ABOUT 5 CUPS

Lotus roots, a common vegetable in Chinese cooking, can be stir-fried, boiled, braised, or added to soups (think of them as a potato substitute), and they're packed with vitamin C and potassium to boot. The lotus plant also carries much spiritual symbolism: for Buddhists, the lotus flower, which floats above muddy waters, represents purity and freedom from attachment and desire. (As such, deities of Asian religions are often depicted as seated on a lotus blossom.) Here I turn the roots into an enlightened chip, which is my favorite way to eat this gorgeous vegetable.

Chinese five-spice powder is available at many groceries, but it is easy to make at home.

MAKE THE FIVE-SPICE POWDER: Heat a small dry skillet over medium heat. Add the star anise, peppercorns, fennel seeds, cloves, and cinnamon stick and toast for 2 to 3 minutes, until you smell the fragrance of the spices. Remove the pan from the heat and set it aside to cool slightly. Then grind the spices with a mortar and pestle or in a spice grinder, until the mixture has the texture of coarsely ground peppercorns. (This will make about ¼ cup of five-spice powder; reserve the extra in a small jar in your pantry for up to 6 months.)

MAKE THE LOTUS ROOT CHIPS: Fill a medium bowl with cool water and stir the lemon juice into it. Peel the lotus root with a vegetable peeler, and then cut it into ⅛-inch-thick rounds. (A mandoline comes in quite handy for this.) Soak the slices in the lemon water for about 15 minutes. Then drain and pat dry. Mix the salt with 1 teaspoon of the spice powder in a small bowl.

FOR THE FIVE-SPICE POWDER:

2 whole **star anise**

1 teaspoon whole **Sichuanese peppercorns**

2½ teaspoons **fennel seeds**

6 whole **cloves**

1 2-inch piece **cinnamon stick**

FOR THE LOTUS ROOT CHIPS:

3 tablespoons fresh **lemon juice**

1 pound fresh **lotus root** (about 1 large root)

1 teaspoon **salt**

Vegetable oil, for frying

**FIERY EDAMAME
WITH GARLIC MISO**
Page 59

Pour the vegetable oil into a medium pot to a depth of 2 inches. Heat the oil until it reaches 325°F on a deep-frying thermometer. Using a slotted spoon, lower the the lotus chips into the frying oil, in small batches, until golden, about 1 minute. As they are cooked, transfer the chips to a paper towel–lined plate to drain. While each batch is still hot, sprinkle it with some of the five-spice salt. Eat right away or store in an airtight jar for up to a week.

TEA-SMOKED EGGS

MAKES 6 EGGS

A great any-time snack, tea eggs can be found at night markets, convenience stores, and even gas stations all across Asia. You'll usually find them kept hot in an electric pot near the cash register at 7-Elevens from Taipei to Tokyo—right next to the displays of Kit Kats, cigarettes, and whiskey. It's the Asian version of the hard-boiled eggs that Parisians grab at Metro stations and café bars, but instead of salt and pepper, these eggs are flavored with smoky tea and the savory goodness of soy sauce, star anise, and orange peel.

6 large **eggs**

¼ cup **dark soy sauce**

1 tablespoon **black tea leaves** (smoky teas, like Lapsang Souchong, are best)

4 **star anise pods**

3 strips fresh **orange peel**

1 tablespoon **whole black peppercorns**

Place the eggs in a saucepan that is large enough to hold them in a single layer. Add enough water to cover the eggs by an inch, bring it to a boil, and cook for 2 minutes, just to lightly set the egg whites.

Drain the eggs and rinse them under cold running water. Gently tap each egg on the countertop, rolling it carefully to lightly crack the surface without breaking it open.

Return the cracked eggs to the pot and just cover them with fresh water. Add the soy sauce, tea leaves, star anise, orange peel, and peppercorns. Bring to a boil. Then reduce the heat to just a simmer, cover the pot, and simmer the eggs for 2 hours.

Remove the pot from the heat and let the eggs cool in the cooking liquid. Then put the pot in the refrigerator and let them steep overnight. Peel when ready to eat or refrigerate for up to a week.

SEAWEED WITH CUCUMBER AND DAIKON RIBBONS

Sunomono

SERVES 6

Just as dried fish makes a popular Asian snack, so too does seaweed, which lines the snack aisle of many Asian grocery stores. With *sunomono,* a distinctive Japanese dish, seaweed is reconstituted and mixed with ribbons of cucumber and daikon. Tossed with a *sanbai-zu* dressing that is equal parts soy sauce, rice vinegar, and mirin, this *sunomono* salad is part of the *izakaya* repertoire.

In Japan there is a seemingly endless array of seaweed, each with its own name and uses. Seaweed is harvested seasonally from the waters surrounding the Japanese archipelago, and the Japanese eat an enormous amount of this alkaline, nutrient-dense food, from nori (mainly used for sushi but also great out of the bag as a crunchy snack) and kanten (a.k.a. agar-agar, a vegetarian gelatin substitute) to kombu (perhaps the king of seaweeds, used for making umami-rich dashi). Wakame, used here, is a type of seaweed that is often found in soups and salads.

3 tablespoons **dried wakame seaweed**

½ large **Japanese daikon**, about 3 inches in diameter

3 medium **Japanese** or **Persian cucumbers**

2 teaspoons **sea salt**

3 tablespoons **rice vinegar**

3 tablespoons **soy sauce**

3 tablespoons **mirin**

Rehydrate the wakame by soaking the seaweed in a large bowl of water for about 1 hour. Use a vegetable peeler to peel and then create ribbons from both the daikon and the cucumbers, and place the ribbons in a medium bowl. Sprinkle the sea salt over the vegetables and let stand for a few minutes, so the salt can draw out the excess water.

In a separate bowl, mix together the rice vinegar, soy sauce, and mirin. Drain the rehydrated wakame and squeeze out the excess water. Drain off any accumulated water in the bowl of cucumbers and daikon and add the wakame. Pour the dressing over the vegetables and toss to mix. Serve at room temperature or chilled.

JAPANESE FRIED CHICKEN

Karaage

SERVES 6

I know very few people who don't like fried chicken, and almost none who can resist chicken *karaage*. These nugget-size bites also taste great cold, so I usually make a big batch, enough for the next day's after-school snack. They are just as tasty with beer at an *izakaya* as they are at a picnic on a sunny day. The last time I made this was for a potluck with old college friends where, as luck would have it, everyone brought fried chicken. I traded some of my chicken *karaage* for some of my friend Welly's Carolina-style buttermilk fried chicken. We drank rosé straight from the bottle and sat back to marvel at our luck of having lots of fried chickens and lots of old friends.

2 tablespoons minced fresh **ginger**

4 **garlic cloves**, minced

½ cup **soy sauce**

¼ cup **sake**

2 tablespoons **sugar**

3 pounds boneless, skin-on **chicken thighs**, cut into 1-inch pieces

1½ cups **potato starch**

Vegetable oil, for frying

Ketchup, for dipping

Lemon wedges, for serving

In a large bowl, mix together the ginger, garlic, soy sauce, sake, and sugar. Add the chicken and mix to combine. Cover the bowl and refrigerate for at least 1 hour or as long as overnight.

Put the potato starch in a large wide bowl. In batches and using tongs, slightly shake off the liquid seasoning and add the chicken pieces to the potato starch, tossing to coat evenly.

Pour the vegetable oil into a wide, deep skillet to a depth of 1 inch. Heat the oil over medium-high heat until a small piece of batter fries and floats upon contact. In batches, fry the chicken until the outside is crispy brown and the chicken is cooked through, about 5 minutes per batch. As they are cooked, transfer the chicken pieces to a paper towel–lined plate to absorb any excess oil.

To double-fry it for added crunch, allow the chicken to cool slightly (at least 5 minutes), and then re-fry it in the same oil for another 5 minutes or so, until the skin is fully browned. Serve with ketchup for dipping and lemon wedges for squeezing over the chicken bites.

★★ NOTE

Karaage is a Japanese cooking technique that's similar to tempura. Do as the Japanese and dip these in ketchup for a Western flair.

GRILLED SARDINES IN SOY SAUCE

SERVES 6

Dried seafood snacks—from shredded squid to salted fish—are perhaps the Asian version of Western snacks like Pop-Tarts and popcorn. And at *izakayas*, little umami-packed fish like sardines are typical snack fare. Alongside edamame, *karaage*, and a bottle of beer, you'll find plenty of these cheap, sustainable, and nutrient-rich fish. They're easy to prepare at home, and cooking them in rice wine and soy sauce takes away any fishiness you might have previously associated with the canned variety. Instead of salt-grilling the sardines, these guys are sautéed in a pan until their bones almost melt. Scoop them up with some of their cooking sauce and eat them over rice.

2 tablespoons **vegetable oil**

18 fresh **sardines**, heads removed (optional), gutted, rinsed, and patted dry

1 1½-inch knob fresh **ginger**, thinly sliced

¼ cup **sake** or other rice cooking wine

¼ cup **soy sauce** (preferably Japanese *shoyu*)

1 **lemon**, thinly sliced

Heat the vegetable oil in a large skillet over medium heat. Add the sardines to the skillet, nestle the ginger slices in between them, and sauté for several minutes, until they start to brown on the bottom. Add the sake and let the pan liquids simmer, shaking the pan gently so the sardines do not stick, for 5 minutes. Then add the soy sauce and continue to simmer for 3 to 4 minutes, until the sauce is mostly reduced and thickened.

Transfer the sardines immediately to a serving plate. Top the sardines with the pan sauce, including the cooked ginger, and scatter the lemon slices over the plate.

HAWAIIAN TUNA POKE

SERVES 6 AS AN APPETIZER

One of Hawaii's favorite fast foods, ready-made poke is available at most local delis. When we were on Kauai to celebrate my mother-in-law Joan's seventieth birthday, one of our best meals was not at a fancy restaurant but at a small deli near Kilauea. Built on the grounds of a former infirmary where Joan's father used to work, this small shop's seafood counter sold some of the most gorgeous tuna loins I had ever seen—exactly what you want for preparing poke. The word *poke* comes from the Hawaiian verb meaning "to slice and cut," which is all you need to do to the tuna to prepare it. For a taste of Hawaii when I'm on the island of Manhattan, I get the freshest tuna I can find and use it as a canvas for a variety of spices and nuts.

1 pound **sashimi-grade ahi tuna steaks**, cut into ½-inch dice

½ cup **soy sauce**

4 **scallions** (green and white parts), thinly sliced

2 tablespoons **Asian sesame oil**

2 tablespoons minced fresh **ginger**

1 tablespoon **toasted sesame seeds**

2 tablespoons chopped **macadamia nuts**, toasted (optional)

Sea salt, to taste

In a large bowl, combine the tuna, soy sauce, scallions, sesame oil, ginger, sesame seeds, and macadamia nuts if using. Gently mix the ingredients, and season with sea salt to taste. Cover the poke with plastic wrap and refrigerate for 30 to 60 minutes before serving.

Poke is usually served as an appetizer or a side dish. To create a heartier snack, scoop a mound of steamed rice (about ½ cup) onto each plate and crown it with an equal amount of poke. For a flourish, finish with a sprinkling of *furikake* seasoning (seaweed with spices, readily available at Japanese groceries) on top.

THE RAMEN REVOLUTION

If there's one dish that defines the ever-shifting Asian food zeitgeist at this particular moment, it's ramen. This humble Japanese noodle soup has taken the food world by storm, creating an obsession that inspires legions of fans to stand in line for hours—come rain, snow, or sleet—for a chance to slurp down a pricey bowl of noodles. How did we suddenly develop a hunger for something that most of us grew up eating from a Styrofoam cup as a last-resort cheap eat? I believe that a perfect storm—involving some very delicious bowls of noodle soup, sprinkled with a smattering of celebrity chefs and crowned by our hunger to consume Asian pop culture through food—set the stage for ramen's meteoric rise to fame. Compounded by social media, where a bowl of ramen is the ultimate food porn, consumer insight has validated what we've known all along: that we'd rather spend our money at the new *ramen-ya* (ramen shop) than splurge on new shoes or concert tickets.

Until a few years ago, most of us probably thought of instant noodles when it came to ramen: fuel for late-night studying in college dorms or hangover grub. But the humble dish quickly ascended the culinary pyramid, thanks in great part to the inventiveness of American chefs for whom ramen was a blank canvas primed for innovation . . . and innovate they did, creating vegetarian ramens, ramen mac-and-cheese, ramen burgers, even ramen-rittos. This everyday fare has been elevated into a chef-driven *cuisine*. A few years ago, there were only a handful of ramen chefs in culinary cities like New York. Now there's one on every block, and their shops are still impossible to get into. Anytown, USA: a *ramen-ya* is coming soon near you.

Back in Japan, where ramen originated as a Chinese noodle (in Japan, ramen is actually thought of as a Chinese dish), ramen *otakus* (obsessive fans) have filled the Internet with documentation of their every sip and slurp. More widespread than even pizzerias and burger joints in the United States, *ramen-yas* dot Japan, each one serving up its signature dish—often a reflection of a regional specialty, like miso ramen from Sapporo in the north or *tonkotsu* ramen in the southern Kyushu region. Unlike other Japanese cuisines that follow a prescribed set of rules (like traditional Japanese *kaiseki* cuisine or sushi), ramen has no rules—including when you eat it, whether as an after-school snack or to satisfy midnight munchies—and that is part of its appeal. Ramen fuels our appetite for innovation just as it feeds our fascination with Asian pop culture.

TONKOTSU RAMEN

SERVES 8

The opposite of instant ramen, *tonkotsu*, this old-school milky pork bone–style broth takes some work and quite a lot of time. But don't let that scare you away—it is well worth the effort. The collagen-rich broth really needs to cook for a good 12 hours to properly extract the milkiness of the bones, but I've streamlined the recipe as much as possible, simplifying it to a good broth with roasted pork belly (*chashu*), a soft-boiled egg, and an optional drizzle of black garlic oil (*mayu*). As for the ramen, I do as most chefs do, and buy my noodles.

MAKE THE BROTH: Put the pigs' feet, chicken, and pork bones in a large stockpot and add cold water to cover. Bring to a boil over high heat, then continue cooking at low heat. Skim off any scum that appears during the first 30 minutes. (Use moist paper towels to wipe any scum from around the rim of the pot.)

Add the onion, garlic, ginger, leeks, scallion whites, and shiitakes and bring back to a boil. Reduce the heat so the stock is barely at a simmer, and cover the pot. Simmer for at least 4 hours, but preferably 10 to 12 hours, topping up with more water when necessary to keep the ingredients covered.

Strain the broth through a fine-mesh strainer into a clean pot, and discard the solids. (You can skim the liquid fat from the top at this time, but it's better to chill the stock overnight and discard the solidified fat afterward.) Salt and pepper the broth to your liking. If not chilling the broth overnight, set it aside while you make the pork belly.

recipe continues

FOR THE RAMEN BROTH:

2 **pigs' feet**, cut crosswise into 1-inch-thick disks

2 pounds **chicken backs and carcasses**, skin and excess fat removed

2 pounds **pork leg bones**, quartered in order to fit into the stockpot

1 large **onion**, skin on, coarsely chopped

12 **garlic cloves**, skin on

1 3-inch knob fresh **ginger**, coarsely chopped

2 **whole leeks** (white and light green parts), coarsely chopped

2 bunches **scallions**, white parts only (reserve green parts for garnish)

6 **dried shiitake mushrooms**

Kosher salt and freshly **ground white pepper**, to taste

COOK THE PORK BELLY: Preheat the oven to 275°F. Combine the soy sauce, mirin, sake, sugar, miso, scallions, garlic, ginger, and shallot with 1 cup of water in a medium ovenproof saucepan, and bring to a boil over high heat. Add the pork belly and cover the pan loosely, with the lid left slightly ajar. Transfer the saucepan to the oven and cook, turning the pork occasionally in the liquid, for 3 to 4 hours, until the pork is completely tender. Let the pork cool completely in its cooking liquid.

SERVE THE RAMEN: While the pork belly is cooling, soft-boil the eggs: Bring a small saucepan of water to a boil, carefully slip in the eggs, and cook for exactly 7 minutes. Remove with a slotted spoon and instantly cool them under cold running water to stop the cooking. When they are cool enough to handle, carefully peel the eggs—they will be soft but will hold their shape. Set aside.

Lift out the cooked pork belly, reserving the liquid in the pot, and cut it into ¼-inch-thick slices. Cover and set aside. Submerge the peeled eggs gently in the cooled pork cooking liquid and let them soak for 2 to 3 hours.

When you are ready to serve the ramen, bring the reserved broth to a boil.

Bring a large pot of water to a boil and cook the ramen noodles according to the package directions.

For each diner, put a serving of noodles in the bottom of a large soup bowl and top it with the hot broth. Slice each egg in half (carefully, as the yolk will be soft). Lay 2 slices of pork belly and an egg half on top of the ramen, and sprinkle liberally with sliced scallion greens. If you like, add some nori strips and enoki mushrooms. Serve at once, with *mayu* if desired.

FOR THE PORK BELLY (*CHASHU*):

½ cup **soy sauce**

1 cup **mirin**

1 cup **sake**

2 tablespoons **sugar**

2 tablespoons **miso paste**

6 **scallions** (green and white parts), coarsely chopped

6 **garlic cloves**

1 2-inch knob fresh **ginger**, coarsely sliced

1 **shallot**, skin on, halved

2 pounds **boneless pork belly**, skin on, boned, rolled, and tied (your butcher will do this)

FOR SERVING:

4 large **eggs**

1½ pounds **ramen noodles**

Reserved **scallion greens**, thinly sliced

Dried nori, cut into ¼-inch-wide strips (optional)

Fresh enoki mushrooms (optional)

Mayu (black garlic oil; optional)

BUBBLE TEA

Boba Cha

SERVES 4

The first time I had bubble tea was at a night market in Taipei, but since then the tapioca pearl tea craze has expanded into seemingly every nook and cranny—like fro-yo shops on caffeine. The pop culture surrounding bubble tea parlors is just as sugary, from the cute bleached blond Taiwanese girls working the cash register to the K-pop music they're bopping to. Born in Taiwan in the 1980s, this drink has earned itself legions of fans who now take their bubble tea with endless variations—fresh fruits, milk, and of course, tapioca pearls. Though the sweet, chewy balls look like bubbles, the name for the drink actually comes from an anglicized form of the Chinese word *boba*, slang for the large tapioca balls that are my favorite part.

1 cup dried large **tapioca pearls**
 (see Note)
1½ cups packed **light brown sugar**
6 **black tea bags**
¼ cup **sweetened condensed milk**

In a large saucepan, bring 2 quarts of water to a rolling boil over high heat. Add the tapioca pearls, stirring with a wooden spoon to prevent them from sticking together. Reduce the heat to medium and simmer gently for up to 30 minutes (depending on how soft you prefer the tapioca balls to be), stirring occasionally. Drain the tapioca pearls into a colander and rinse them under cool running water.

In a medium saucepan, combine the brown sugar with 1 cup of water and cook over medium heat, stirring, for 5 to 6 minutes, until the sugar has dissolved. Drain the tapioca bubbles and add them to the brown sugar syrup.

Bring 4 cups of water to a boil in another saucepan over high heat. Add the tea bags, remove from the heat, and allow to steep for 4 to 5 minutes. Divide among the glasses.

** NOTE

Tapioca pearls can be purchased either fresh or dried. Dried pearls will need to be cooked before serving.

To assemble each bubble tea, put ¼ cup of the bubbles and a few tablespoons of the sugar syrup in the bottom of each serving glass. Fill a cocktail shaker halfway with ice cubes, and add 1 cup of the hot tea and 1 tablespoon of the sweetened condensed milk for each serving. Cap and shake vigorously until the hot tea is chilled (the outside of the shaker will feel cold). Pour the cold tea over the bubbles and serve at once, adding more ice to the glass if desired.

SNACKS AND GRUB

SOUPS AND BROTHS

THAI SHRIMP BOIL
AND SOUP

Page 85

Knowing how to make a good soup holds a special place of pride among many Chinese cooks, whose mastery of cooking is tested by preparing deceptively simple dishes such as the soups in this chapter. Dishes like these are what separate a chef from a cook—not unlike the way the mastery of clear consommés is a rite of passage for earning a classic French toque.

At the humble Asian table, soups vary between ordinary and extraordinary, but they are an integral part of most meals, especially home-cooked ones. What might otherwise be tossed out—neck bones, chicken feet, cilantro stems, turnip tops, and anything cartilaginous and bone-rich—is instead tossed into the pot. These odds and ends are what transform soups into elixirs. As an accompaniment to a meal, rather than as a stand-alone course, such broths are often sipped throughout the meal in lieu of tea or water to cleanse the palate; in the process they add a great deal of nourishment. Recipes like Hot and Sour Soup (page 82) or Herbal Bone Tea Soup (page 93) are what an Asian grandmother might feed you. I feel better before I even have a sip.

I am a believer in the curative powers of soups, both medicinal and spiritual. It's therapy in a bowl, if you will. The ultimate pick-me-up for the body and mind is the intoxicating scent of the delicate fragrance of scallions, ginger, and chicken simmering on the stove. But I'm not alone. Our ancestors across the globe have long treated soups as healing tonics. The Chinese in particular believe that a path to curing a cold is to "sweat it out," and sipping hot soup (especially one that includes ginger, a sweat-inducing herb) certainly seems to help with decongestion, hydration, and a deeper level of healing. Even though doctors may no longer prescribe chicken soup in favor of antibiotics, I find that there are still modern-day ailments—fatigue, stress, over-connectivity—that only an old-fashioned bowl of soup can make better.

Recently there has been a resurgence of popularity in bone broths—athletes are crediting the collagen-rich brew with keeping them nimble and supermodels thank it for their youthful skin. Chefs are even opening broth bars, where you can pick up a cup of bone broth instead of coffee or green juice. What's old is new again.

LONG LIFE "SUPREME" BROTH

MAKES 4 QUARTS, SERVES 8

Cantonese bone broths like this one can be used as a master stock for countless other soups, but they are also amazing on their own and renowned for their restorative properties. Also known as "long life soup," these tonics are brewed with ancient Chinese "secret" ingredients—namely ginger, goji berries, and red dates—that are not-so-secret anymore. I've had home-style versions that are made with artichoke leaves, carrot tops, mushroom stems, and otherwise discarded stems from greens, and I like to add aromatics such as chopped cilantro and scallions. Bones, particularly chicken or pork or a mixture, add depth and richness.

Place the chicken (including head and feet if you have them), pork bones, and ham in a large stockpot, and add water to cover. Bring the water to a boil and then cook just long enough to rinse the meats of scum and fat, about 10 minutes. Discard the water and rinse the meats and the pot.

Return the rinsed meats and bones to the clean pot, and add water to cover by ½ inch. Bring the water to a boil, and then add the ginger, scallions, garlic, onion, goji berries, red dates, and mushrooms. Reduce the heat, cover the pot, and simmer for 2 hours, occasionally skimming any fat off the surface, to produce a finished stock. Strain the stock with a fine-mesh sieve.

Add the Shaoxing rice wine, season with salt and pepper to taste, and serve the soup as part of a meal or with rice and pickles. The soup will also benefit from a garnish of chopped cilantro and scallions.

Store any remaining soup in the refrigerator for up to a week, or in the freezer for about a month.

1 3-pound **chicken**, cut into 8 pieces

1 pound **pork rib bones**

1 ¼-pound slice **Virginia ham** or **slab bacon**

1 2-inch knob fresh **ginger**, smashed and coarsely chopped

1 bunch **scallions** (green and white parts), halved crosswise

6 **garlic cloves**, smashed

1 **yellow onion**, quartered

2 tablespoons **goji berries**

10 **red dates**

6 whole **dried shiitake mushrooms**

Shaoxing rice wine, to taste

Salt and freshly **ground black pepper**

Chopped fresh **cilantro leaves**, for garnish (optional)

Chopped **scallions** (green and white parts), for garnish (optional)

This recipe works with just about any chicken, but see if you can get your hands on a Longgang heritage chicken, available at most Chinese groceries and renowned for its texture and sumptuous taste. It will produce a much more flavorful broth.

DOUBLE-BOILED CHICKEN SOUP

MAKES ABOUT 1 QUART, SERVES 4

This soup is so intense, in terms of both its healing properties and its flavor, that I consider it more of a tonic than a broth. Because of the double-boiling method, the chicken is not submerged in water but rather slowly steams in its own juices. This technique is especially popular in Cantonese cuisine, and beautiful cauldrons that are fitted with a steaming bowl are made specifically for this dish.

This is a very luxurious soup since a whole chicken is used to produce just a few concentrated bowls. Be sure to use the best possible ingredients. I prefer black Silkie chickens, which are found in most Asian groceries for the same price as an organic chicken. These highly prized birds have silky white plumage and stark black skin (and even black bones), and produce a particularly fragrant broth.

1 3-pound **chicken** (black Silkie if available, or free-range), cut into 8 pieces

1 cup **Shaoxing rice wine**

10 thick slices fresh **ginger**, cut in half and smashed

10 **scallions** (green and white parts), halved and smashed

1½ teaspoons **sea salt**, or to taste

Bring a very large stockpot of water to a boil. Add the chicken and blanch it for about 3 minutes to cleanse it. Remove and rinse the chicken; then set it aside in a large heatproof bowl that will fit into the stockpot. Discard the water from the stockpot, add 6 cups of fresh water, and bring it to a boil.

Add the rice wine, ginger, and scallions to the bowl holding the chicken, and place the bowl in the stockpot. (The water should come up around the sides of the bowl, but not spill into it or out of the pot. If you don't have a large enough stockpot, substitute a wide cooking vessel, such as a wok with a lid.) Cover the bowl with a plate, then cover the stockpot, and let the chicken steam in its own juices over high heat for about 3 hours. Replenish the water in the stockpot as needed, so it surrounds the bowl at all times.

Remove the bowl from the stockpot, and lift out the chicken. Skim any residual impurities or fat off the surface of the broth, and

season the broth with the sea salt. Divide the broth among 4 soup
bowls. The chicken flavor (and nutrition) is mostly transferred to
the soup after so many hours of cooking, but if you like, you can
add some of the meat (bone-in) to the soup for texture. The soup
is best consumed right away.

HOT AND SOUR SOUP

Suan La Tong

SERVES 4 TO 6

Hot and sour soups are popular throughout Asia—from the "sour soups" (*canh chua*) of Vietnam to the *tom yum* of Thailand (see page 85). However, thanks to Chinese restaurants, you can find a Westernized version of this soup (and an egg roll!) almost everywhere, best enjoyed with a cheap-and-cheerful takeout box of Beef with Broccoli (see page 126).

This is a home-style hot and sour soup, closer to the way it is served in China. Although most versions use a simple chicken broth, this recipe creates an indulgent version with the luxurious use of Long Life "Supreme" Broth (page 79).

2 ounces (½ cup) **dried wood ear mushrooms**

2 ounces (½ cup) **dried daylilies**

Boiling water

½ pound **boneless pork loin**, cut horizontally into long, 2-inch-thick pieces and then vertically into slivers (freeze briefly for easier cutting)

1 tablespoon **cornstarch**

¼ cup **soy sauce**

4 cups **Long Life "Supreme" Broth** (page 79) or other **chicken broth**

2 tablespoons **vegetable oil**

½ pound **firm tofu**, cut into 2-inch-long slivers

8 fresh **shiitake mushrooms**, thinly sliced

1 6-ounce can sliced **bamboo shoots**, drained

3 large **eggs**, beaten together

1 teaspoon finely ground **white pepper**, or to taste

¼ cup **Chinkiang black vinegar**, or to taste

2 tablespoons **Asian sesame oil**

Thinly sliced **scallions** (green and white parts), for garnish

Chopped fresh **cilantro leaves and stems**, for garnish

Place the dried mushrooms and daylilies in separate bowls, and cover both with boiling water. Soak for 30 minutes to rehydrate.

In a small bowl, toss the pork loin pieces with the cornstarch and soy sauce. Let sit for at least 15 minutes to tenderize the pork. (The cornstarch on the pork will also help to thicken the soup when the pork is added.) Drain the mushrooms and daylilies; thinly slice them both and set aside.

Pour the "Supreme" Broth into a large pot and bring it to a boil.

In a wok, heat the vegetable oil over high heat until sizzling. Add the pork loin and stir-fry for about 2 minutes, until it is lightly browned. Add the wood ear mushrooms, daylilies, tofu, shiitake mushrooms, and bamboo shoots and stir-fry for 2 minutes.

Add the wok ingredients to the broth, return it to a boil over medium heat, and cook for 2 to 3 minutes. Remove the pot from the heat and slowly drizzle in the beaten eggs, stirring constantly. Stir in the white pepper, vinegar, and sesame oil. Serve at once, with sliced scallions and chopped cilantro.

HEALING SOUPS FOR NEW MOMS

After giving birth, many Chinese women abide by an ancient yet still very popular practice called *Zuo Yue-Zi*, which literally means "Sitting Month," or in the rather unappealing English translation, "Month of Confinement." Traditional Chinese medicine believes that the month following childbirth is an essential time for the new mother to rest and restore her own health in order to properly provide for her child. Though there are onerous (and potentially odorous!) rituals involved, such as not bathing or exposing oneself to a cool breeze, the practice happily includes drinking many, many bowls of delicious healing soups such as the Double-Boiled Chicken Soup (page 80).

When I gave birth to my two daughters, my mom convinced me to practice "confinement" just the way she had done after my birth. Even though it may be part myth, part science, the traditional diet that goes into postpartum care makes a whole lot of sense. The practice is based on the theory of dividing foods into "warm" and "cold" categories, with each food linked to a health benefit; for example, eating liver replenishes lost blood, green papaya stimulates milk production, and kidneys help with aches and pains. Dishes are loaded with healing ingredients such as ginger, longan, red dates (to nourish the blood), ginseng, Chinese angelica root, goji berries, and certain meats like black chicken. These ingredients drive away the "wind" element (considered negative in Chinese medicine because "wind" causes movement, imbalance, and instability) and restore balance to the body and the soul.

Healing soups like Korean Seaweed Soup (page 92) are fundamental to the postpartum diet, but such ancient Asian remedies are also tonics for broader health and recovery.

THAI SHRIMP BOIL AND SOUP

Tom Yum Goong

SERVES 6

This two-in-one recipe is great for entertaining: host a festive shrimp boil, then use the shrimp stock for a crock of *tom yum goong* soup. Thai roasted chili paste gives this more of a pronounced Thai flavor. Set up the action by spreading some newspapers on the kitchen table, or at an outdoor picnic table, and then serve the boiled shrimp, allowing guests to discard their shells onto the newspapers. After the boil, you have an excellent base to build upon for the *tom yum goong* soup, or to use for other recipes such as Curry *Laksa* (page 21).

PREPARE THE SHRIMP BOIL: In a large stockpot, bring 10 cups of water to a boil over high heat. Reduce the heat and add the lemongrass, shallots, galangal, chiles, Kaffir lime leaves, coriander, and roasted chili paste. Cover and let simmer for 10 minutes. Just before serving, add the shrimp to the simmering water, remove the pot from the heat, and let sit for 3 minutes to just cook the shrimp through.

Combine the lime juice and fish sauce in a small bowl. Scoop the cooked shrimp from the broth, reserving the cooking liquid in the pot. Put the shrimp on a serving dish (or on a paper-covered table), and serve the dipping sauce alongside.

MAKE THE SOUP: Peel the shrimp, reserving the shells. Bring the reserved broth back to a boil over high heat. Add the shrimp shells and boil lightly for about 30 minutes. Strain the broth and discard the solids. Add the mushrooms to the broth and bring it back to a boil. Add the shrimp and cook for 1 to 2 minutes, until the shrimp are pink and opaque. Remove the pot from the heat and stir in the cilantro and basil. Season with additional fish sauce, lime juice, and roasted chili paste to taste.

FOR THE SHRIMP BOIL:

3 **lemongrass stalks**, trimmed, cut into 4-inch lengths, and smashed

4 **shallots**, smashed

4 large slices fresh **galangal**, smashed

10 whole **dried chiles**, or to taste, pounded

5 fresh **Kaffir lime leaves**, torn into pieces

1 tablespoon **coriander seeds**

3 to 4 tablespoons **Thai roasted chili paste** (*nam prik phao*), plus more for seasoning the finished soup

3 pounds medium **shrimp**, preferably with heads on

Juice of 2 **limes** (about ½ cup), plus more for seasoning the finished soup

¼ cup **fish sauce**, plus more for seasoning the finished soup

FOR THE SOUP:

1 pound medium **shrimp**, preferably with heads on

1 6-ounce can **straw mushrooms**, drained

½ cup chopped fresh **cilantro leaves**

1 cup fresh **Thai holy basil leaves**, hand-torn

SUMO WRESTLERS' STEW

Chanko Nabe

SERVES 1 SUMO WRESTLER OR 4 CIVILIANS

A cousin to the Chinese Hot Pot (page 89), Japanese *nabe* are one-pot meals where a flavored broth provides the basic building block. Known as Sumo Wrestlers' Stew, this *chanko nabe* contains only chicken meat, based on an old superstition that eating two-legged animals helps to keep a person—in this case, a sumo wrestler—on his feet. Since sumo wrestlers are not known for their svelte figures, you may not be tempted to mimic their diet. However, this stew is actually full of broth, healthy, and low-fat. The chicken meatballs (*tsukune*) in this dish are also delicious on their own, grilled and glazed with soy or teriyaki sauce (see page 19). Other soupy Japanese *nabes* of note include *yosenabe* (seafood stew) and *sukiyaki* (a sweet beef and vegetable stew). Typically served in a clay or cast-iron pot (because they evenly distribute and retain heat), *nabes* are placed at the center of the dining table so that everyone can serve themselves from the same pot.

In a medium bowl, mix together the ground chicken, scallions, miso, and salt. Cover and refrigerate for about 30 minutes; then shape the mixture into about a dozen small meatballs. Set aside.

Bring the dashi to a simmer in a large pot. Stir in the soy sauce, mirin, and sake. Add the chicken thighs, chicken meatballs, daikon, carrots, and potatoes and cook for 15 minutes. Add the shiitake and enoki mushrooms, cabbage, leeks, and tofu puffs and cook until all the ingredients are cooked through, about 10 minutes.

Add the cooked udon noodles and cook until just heated through.

Add more soy sauce or miso paste to taste, and serve table-side in one pot or divide among individual bowls.

1 pound **ground chicken**

4 **scallions** (light green and white parts), minced

¼ cup **white miso paste**, plus more for serving

1 tablespoon **salt**

8 cups **dashi** (see Note)

¼ cup **soy sauce**, plus more for serving

2 tablespoons **mirin**

¼ cup **sake**

1 pound boneless, skinless **chicken thighs**, cut into 1-inch pieces

1 large **daikon**, cut into 1-inch pieces

2 large **carrots**, cut into 1-inch pieces

2 large **potatoes**, cut into 1-inch pieces

10 fresh **shiitake mushrooms**, halved

1 bunch fresh **enoki mushrooms**, trimmed

½ head **napa cabbage**, cut into 1-inch pieces

3 **Japanese leeks** (*negi*), or 2 leeks (white and light green parts), cut diagonally into 1-inch slices

8 **fried tofu puffs**, halved (found in most Asian grocers)

1 pound **udon noodles**, cooked

★ ★
NOTE Dashi is a Japanese stock made from soaking dried
seaweed and shaved bonito flakes. You can find it at
Asian grocery stores or just substitute chicken broth.

MISO CLAM SOUP

SERVES 6

If you know how to boil water, you're halfway to making miso soup. It's that simple: add miso paste to hot water and stir. Although traditional miso soup is made with dashi, a broth seasoned with the dried seaweed kombu and bonito fish flakes, I also like making a quick version with just hot water and some good miso paste. Instead of tea, I like to make a mug of miso soup and enjoy it with a bowl of rice for breakfast. This recipe notches up the luxe factor with the addition of briny Manila clams, but is still simple to make.

Miso is essentially soybeans that are fermented with a mold known as *koji*. It can ferment in as little as 3 days or as long as 3 years, yielding miso that varies in complexity, color, and flavor. My favorite type is salty red miso from Japan's northern port of Hokkaido, but other varieties of miso such as the sweet white miso from Kyoto also make delicious miso soup.

In a large pot, bring 6 cups of water to a boil. Add the tofu and ginger, and bring back to a gentle boil. Add the clams, cover the pot, and cook until the clams have opened up, about 3 minutes. (Discard any that do not open.)

Turn off the heat and stir in the miso to dissolve it, adding more to taste if you like. Top each serving with chopped scallions and shredded nori.

1 pound **soft ("silken") tofu**, cut into
½-inch cubes

4 thin slices fresh **ginger**

1 pound small **Manila clams**,
scrubbed and debearded

¼ cup **red miso paste**, plus more to
taste

Chopped **scallions** (green and white
parts), for serving

Roasted nori, shredded, for serving

Never boil miso as it will become gritty.

HOT POT

Huo Guo

SERVES 6 TO 8

At times referred to as "Chinese fondue" (*huo guo* means "fire pot"), a hot pot is an interactive experience where everyone gets to play chef. In my family, these convivial feasts are popular during holidays when we all gather around a giant pot of boiling soup and platters of raw meats, seafood, vegetables, and delicacies and cook, eat, and chat until our bellies feel as though they're about to pop, our faces are flushed, and the windows have fogged up with the steam emanating from the pot. My favorite part comes at the end, when we drink the broth that is the layered result of everything that went into the soup. It's a true melting pot, and the only part of the meal when everyone is eating the same thing.

There are endless variations on hot pots—the Sichuanese create a numbingly spicy broth (*ma la huo guo*) with peppercorns bobbing in the chili oil–laden soup and the Japanese have *shabu shabu*, named for the sound of the beef as it is cooking in the hot liquid. If you can't decide which to serve, consider purchasing a hot pot that is divided into two sections to make the romantic-sounding Lover's Hot Pot (*Yuan Yang Huo Guo*).

SOAK THE NOODLES: Put the mung bean noodles in a bowl and cover them with cold water. Let sit for 30 minutes to soften; then drain and set aside.

MEANWHILE, SET THE TABLE: Arrange all the hot pot ingredients and the dipping sauce ingredients (except the eggs) in individual small bowls or platters in the center of the table. Place a rice bowl at each guest's place, and beat an egg in each bowl.

recipe continues

FOR THE NOODLES:

1 1-pound package **mung bean vermicelli noodles**

FOR THE HOT POT INGREDIENTS:

2 pounds **beef**, sliced paper thin (nearly any kind of beef will work here, but fatty, marbled cuts are preferred)

½ pound **razor clams** or **littleneck clams**

½ pound medium **shrimp**, heads on, peel and deveined

½ pound **mixed fish cakes** (I recommend white pollock balls, which can be found frozen in most Asian grocers)

½ pound **mixed fresh mushrooms** (such as shiitakes, enokis, and beech mushrooms)

½ pound **mixed leafy greens** (such as chrysanthemum greens, spinach, and watercress)

PREPARE THE BROTH: Fill a pot halfway with water and bring it to a boil on a hot plate or table-top gas burner. When the water boils, add the ginger and scallions. When the water returns to a boil, the hot pot is ready to go!

Each guest selects the dipping sauces and flavorings they like, and stirs them into the beaten egg in their bowl. Using chopsticks or a small metal strainer, each guest then dips their choice of meat, seafood, and/or vegetables into the hot broth. (The meat should be swirled in the hot water until it is just cooked, 3 to 5 seconds.) Then dip each cooked item into the individual bowl of sauce before eating.

At the end of the meal, add the reserved vermicelli noodles to the broth and boil until just cooked, about 5 minutes. Dish the noodles and broth into serving bowls, and season each bowl to taste with the remaining dipping sauces.

 ★ ★ NOTE Part of the charm of hot pots is how open-ended they are; I've included my favorite ingredients here, but feel free to substitute your own.

FOR THE DIPPING SAUCES:

½ cup *sha cha sauce* (a Taiwanese fermented brill **fish sauce**)

½ cup minced fresh **cilantro leaves**

½ cup minced **scallions** (light green and white parts)

½ cup **Asian sesame oil**

½ cup **soy sauce**

½ cup **chili paste**

6 to 8 large **eggs** (1 per person)

FOR THE BROTH:

1 1-inch knob fresh **ginger**, smashed

1 bunch **scallions** (green and white parts), sliced diagonally

Perfect Steamed Rice, (page 145), for serving

KOREAN SEAWEED SOUP

Miyeokguk

SERVES 4

When I have a food craving—whether it's for fried chicken or kale salad—I try to allow my body to lead the way. Luckily, much of what I crave, like this vitamin-packed seaweed soup, is also healthy and healing. In Korean culture, this soup is a must for new mothers. Seaweed, a great source of calcium, iodine, fiber, omega acids, and vitamins B1 and B3, has innumerable postpartum health benefits such as metabolism regulation, blood purification, constipation relief, and detoxification. Instead of plain water, nutrient-packed milky, rice-washed water is used to enrich the soup. Because this soup is a rite of passage for new mothers, Koreans also eat it on birthdays to commemorate their mothers, as birthdays are always a day to celebrate mom!

1 ounce **dried wakame seaweed**

2 cups uncooked **short- or medium-grain rice**

1 tablespoon **Asian sesame oil**, plus more for seasoning

1 tablespoon chopped **garlic**

9 ounces **beef stew meat**, cubed

1 tablespoon **sea salt**

1 tablespoon **soy sauce**

Rinse the seaweed thoroughly under cool running water. Then submerge it in a bowl of cool water and leave it for at least 30 minutes, until it has softened. Drain well and set aside.

Combine the rice with 8 cups of water in a large bowl, and stir together. Then drain the rice through a sieve set over another large bowl, catching the milky water in the bowl. Set the drained rice aside to use in another dish.

Heat the sesame oil in a large pot set over medium heat. Add the garlic, and stir-fry for about 30 seconds, until fragrant. Add the beef and stir-fry until it is cooked through, about 3 minutes. Add the drained seaweed and sauté for another 3 minutes.

Add the reserved rice water, the sea salt, and soy sauce. Bring to a boil and cook, uncovered, for about 30 minutes, skimming the fat from the surface as it cooks, and reducing the liquid to concentrate the soup's nutritional impact. Drizzle additional sesame oil onto each portion before serving.

HERBAL BONE TEA SOUP

Bak Kut Teh

SERVES 6

This pork rib soup is made with medicinal herbs such as angelica root and Sichuanese lovage rhizome—herbs that are credited with healing everything from insomnia to menstrual cramps. The soup is as dark as black tea, thanks to the soy sauces, and is a favorite tonic of mine perhaps because it tastes, well, medicinal, and reminiscent of the Chinese medicinal herbal teas I drank as a child whenever I had a cold. It is popular throughout Singapore and Malaysia, where many restaurants have proprietary locks on their recipes. I like to make mine in a Chinese herb cooking pot, which has a spout like a teapot, and to serve the soup in teacups that can be replenished throughout a meal.

Rehydrate the shiitake mushrooms by soaking them in a bowl of warm water for 30 minutes or until softened.

Place the pork ribs in a deep soup pot and cover with 8 cups of water. Bring the water to a boil; then reduce the heat and simmer for about 15 minutes, occasionally skimming the debris and scum from the surface. Add the angelica root, lovage rhizome, garlic, cinnamon stick, star anise, cloves, goji berries, and drained shiitake mushrooms. Add the soy sauces, salt, and sugar. Cover the pot and simmer for about 1 hour, until the pork is cooked through and tender. Strain the soup, reserving the pork ribs.

Place the pork ribs on a cutting board. Cut the meat away from the bone; chop the meat and return it to the soup before serving.

8 **dried shiitake mushrooms**

1 pound **baby back pork ribs**

¼ cup **dried angelica root**

2 tablespoons **Sichuanese lovage rhizome granules**

1 head **garlic**, cloves lightly smashed

1 1-inch piece **cinnamon stick**

1 **star anise pod**

5 **whole cloves**

2 tablespoons **dried whole goji berries**

2 tablespoons **dark soy sauce**

2 tablespoons **light soy sauce**

1 teaspoon **salt**

1 tablespoon **sugar**

Many of the medicinal herbs called for in this recipe are available packaged together in Asian groceries, and can also be found in homeopathic pharmacies. For a simple, nurturing meal when you're under the weather, serve this soup with rice (and perhaps some wok-fried greens).

SPICY DISHES

CURRY IN A HURRY
Page 109

Burn-your-face-off curries, mouth-numbing peppercorns, nostril-clearing wasabi: such are the lore (and lure) of Asian food. In truth, the vast majority of Asian dishes are not spicy, but some very famous ones that are spicy have solidified the cuisine's *hot-hot-hot* reputation—and perhaps intimidated the uninitiated.

I am such a fan of fiery foods that when guests tell me they don't like it, I feel a momentary surge of panic. Sooner or later, compromises will have to be made—I imagine, at the dinner table where spice levels will need to be tempered. I understand that everyone's appetite and tolerance for spice varies, but I can't help pitying folks who never give spice a chance . . . because I was once a stubborn child with a preference for bland, starchy noodles. It wasn't until I encountered dishes like *Ma Po Tofu* (opposite) that I started to develop powerful cravings for *mala* peppercorns (ground Sichuanese peppercorns) and broad bean paste. It feels torturously good to shovel in mouthful after mouthful until the spice coats the back of my throat—almost like an anesthetic—allowing me to eat more.

If Asia is a food lover's dream come true, then China's Sichuan province is a spice addict's opium den. When I traveled there I found it unusual that, even during the summer evenings when the temperature reached the high 90s, local folks would sit by the river and eat a bubbling-hot Spicy Fish Stew (page 112). It sounds counterintuitive, but in fact it makes perfect sense: when it's hot outside, eating spicy foods induces sweating, which in turn cools the body as the perspiration evaporates. But even though fiery seasonings like tingly peppercorns are a hallmark of Sichuanese cooking, this sophisticated cuisine is actually renowned for its delicacy and balance of flavors. (In fact, heat is just one beloved property of spice, which can add pungency, zest, and even sweetness to foods.)

The spice-heavy dishes in this chapter now appear in many of my daydreams. I only wish I had tried them earlier! Thanks to fiery foods, I've discovered a brave new world that has only increased my appetite for the spices that lured so many caravans along the Silk Road.

MA PO TOFU

SERVES 6

Now a hallmark of many Chinese restaurant menus, this legendary Sichuanese dish is named after a pockmarked (*ma*) old lady (*po*) who is said to have created the recipe. Though it contains meat, this dish is popular among vegetarians (by omitting the meat) and beautifully showcases the tofu and bean paste responsible for its distinct flavor. The flavor and spiciness of *ma po* tofu is often muted to cater to Western palates, but this more traditional version rewards spice lovers with the full spectrum of heat—without going overboard and interfering with the flavor balance.

In a small bowl, stir the ground pork with the cornstarch and soy sauce. Let marinate for 10 minutes.

Heat the vegetable oil in a wok set over medium-high heat. Add the garlic and ginger and cook for 30 seconds, until the garlic is fragrant. Add the marinated pork and stir-fry for 3 to 4 minutes, until it is just cooked through.

Add the bean paste and the Sichuanese peppercorns; stir-fry for 1 minute. Then add the chicken broth, bring it to a simmer, and immediately add the tofu. Cook for 2 to 3 minutes to heat through. Sprinkle the scallions on top, and serve at once with hot rice on the side.

½ pound **ground pork**

2 tablespoons **cornstarch**

2 tablespoons **soy sauce**

2 tablespoons **vegetable oil**

2 **garlic cloves**, minced

1 1-inch knob fresh **ginger**, minced

2 tablespoons **chili bean paste** (*doubanjiang*)

1 teaspoon freshly **ground Sichuanese peppercorns**

½ cup **chicken broth**

1 pound **soft ("silken") tofu**, cut into 1-inch cubes

4 **scallions** (green and white parts), thinly sliced

Perfect Steamed Rice (page 145), for serving

OCTOPUS WITH WASABI

Tako Wasabi

SERVES 4 AS AN APPETIZER

An unlikely couple, chewy raw octopus and fresh wasabi are made for each other; the combination satisfies those spice cravings I often get. Fresh wasabi stem, or Japanese horseradish, has a heat that's more like mustard than like a chile pepper. It hits the nasal passages more than the sensory receptors on the tongue. Unfortunately, fresh wasabi is hard to find outside of Japan, though some farmers are now cultivating it in California and elsewhere as the demand increases. A common substitute for grated fresh wasabi—even in well-respected sushi restaurants—is actually a blend of horseradish, mustard powder, and green food coloring. If you can find real wasabi, use it right away after grating it, as prepared wasabi actually loses flavor after about 15 minutes—hence sushi chefs' practice of dabbing it between the fish and the rice to preserve its pungency.

Put the fresh octopus on a plate, and chill it in the freezer until it is frozen (this process kills potential parasites). Slightly defrost just before preparing the dish; partially frozen octopus will be easier to cut.

Place the diced cucumber in a colander, sprinkle the salt over it, and let it sit at room temperature for about 5 minutes to drain it of excess water.

Meanwhile, combine the soy sauce, sugar, rice vinegar, sake, and wasabi in a small bowl to make the vinaigrette. Set aside.

Dice the lightly frozen octopus into ½-inch chunks. Let the chunks thaw; then rinse them under cold running water and pat them dry.

To serve, mix the octopus, cucumber, and vinaigrette in a bowl, and divide it among 4 small plates.

1 cup fresh **raw octopus** (see Note)

1 **Japanese or Persian cucumber**, unpeeled, halved lengthwise and cut into ½-inch dice

1 teaspoon **salt**

2 tablespoons **soy sauce**

1 tablespoon **sugar**

1 tablespoon **rice vinegar**

1 tablespoon **sake**

1 tablespoon grated **fresh wasabi** (if fresh wasabi is not available, substitute prepared wasabi from a tube, found in Asian groceries)

★ ★
NOTE

If you can find fresh baby octopus, this is the best option. If raw octopus is not an option, you can substitute canned cooked octopus, available at most Spanish groceries.

THAI GRILLED BEEF SALAD

Yam Neua Yang

SERVES 6

Grilled beef salad is usually a crowd-pleaser, and this Thai version hits all the high notes: smoky, beefy, spicy, herbal, sweet, salty, citrusy. I like to toss in copious amounts of mint, basil, and cilantro to create a robust salad that almost competes with the meat. Flank steak, grilled to medium-rare and then thinly sliced, works well for meatiness and uniformity. Best of all, everything is served at room temperature, so this dish is perfect for a summer potluck.

In a small bowl, combine the 3 tablespoons of fish sauce with the 1 tablespoon of lime juice and smashed garlic. Place the flank steak in a shallow dish, and pour the marinade evenly over it. Cover, and marinate at room temperature for at least 30 minutes, until the meat comes to room temperature.

Prepare a hot grill, or preheat a stovetop grill pan. Remove the meat from the marinade, and grill it for 4 to 5 minutes per side, until it's well seared on the outside and firm to the touch, but still very pink in the center. Let the meat rest on a cutting board for 10 minutes.

While the meat rests, combine the cucumbers, tomatoes, red onion, basil, cilantro, and mint in a medium bowl. Toss with a sprinkling of sea salt to draw out the liquid. Discard the liquid.

In a separate bowl, combine the remaining lime juice and the fish sauce, the chopped garlic, lemongrass, chiles, and Sriracha if using.

To serve, slice the meat diagonally across the grain into ½-inch-thick slices. Just before serving, gently toss the meat and vegetables with the dressing. Garnish with additional cilantro if desired, and serve at once.

3 tablespoons **fish sauce** for the marinade, plus 6 tablespoons fish sauce for the dressing

5 tablespoons fresh **lime juice**

2 **garlic cloves**, smashed, plus 4 garlic cloves, chopped

2 pounds **flank steak**

2 medium **cucumbers**, halved, seeded, and sliced into half-moons

2 medium **tomatoes**, halved or quartered

1 medium **red onion**, thinly sliced

½ cup chopped fresh **basil leaves**

½ cup chopped fresh **cilantro leaves and stems**, plus more for garnish (optional)

½ cup chopped fresh **mint leaves and stems**

Sea salt, to taste

1 **lemongrass stalk**, trimmed and finely sliced

4 **dried Thai bird's-eye chiles**, coarsely torn, or 1 teaspoon **Thai roasted chili paste**

1 tablespoon **Sriracha**, or to taste (optional)

SICHUANESE CHICKEN WINGS

SERVES 4 TO 6

This take on an American finger food favorite gets its spice from Sichuanese pepper and is stir-fried with aggressive amounts of chiles, which—despite their fiery red appearance—add more flavor than heat. These wings are baked, not fried, but still have a wonderful crunch.

Preheat the oven to 400°F.

Line a large rimmed baking sheet with aluminum foil and spread the chicken wings out on it. Sprinkle them generously with salt. Bake for 45 to 50 minutes, until the wings are golden brown and crisp. Drain off the fat and transfer the wings to a serving bowl.

In a cast-iron skillet set over medium-high heat, toast the red chile flakes, cumin seeds, Sichuanese peppercorns, and star anise, shaking the pan constantly, until the spices are toasty and fragrant, 2 to 3 minutes. Immediately pour them into a bowl to stop the cooking. Cool slightly, and then grind to a powder in a spice grinder or with a mortar and pestle.

In the same dry skillet, toast the dried chiles, shaking the pan constantly, until they darken in color and smell fragrant, 3 minutes.

To serve, toss the wings with the ground spice mixture. Then add the toasted whole chiles and the julienned ginger. Taste, and add more salt if necessary. Sprinkle with the chopped cilantro and serve at once.

3 pounds **chicken wings**, split in half, wing tips removed (optional)

Kosher salt

2 tablespoons crushed **red chile flakes**

2 teaspoons whole **cumin seeds**

1 teaspoon **Sichuanese peppercorns**

1 **star anise pod**

1 cup **dried red Chinese chiles**

1 1-inch knob fresh **ginger**, julienned

¼ cup chopped fresh **cilantro leaves**

SPICY PORK NOODLES

Zha Jiang Mian

SERVES 6

Zha jiang, a salty fermented soybean paste, is the major flavor ingredient in this Chinese spaghetti-like dish, which—like the Italian version—consists of a saucy meat ragù served over wheat noodles. Beyond China, this is also Korea's comfort food (called *jajangmyeon*). Ideal for entertaining, this dish is traditionally served at room temperature and can be assembled at the table by guests according to their individual tastes. If you prefer your noodles less spicy, substitute more hoisin sauce for the traditional soybean paste.

Cook the noodles in a large pot of boiling water according to the package directions; then drain and rinse them under cold running water. Drain the noodles and toss them in a bowl with 1 tablespoon of the sesame oil.

Heat the vegetable oil in a large wok set over medium heat. When the oil is sizzling, add the garlic and stir-fry for 30 seconds, until fragrant. Add the ground pork and stir-fry for 2 minutes, until slightly browned. Add the bean curd, shiitake mushrooms, and bean sprouts and stir-fry for an additional 2 minutes.

In a small bowl, combine the soybean paste and hoisin sauce with the soy sauce and the remaining 2 tablespoons sesame oil. (If the mixture is too thick, add up to ¼ cup water to loosen it.) Pour the mixture into the wok and stir-fry for a minute to combine with the pork and vegetables. Remove from the heat and transfer the meat sauce to a bowl.

Divide the noodles among individual serving bowls. In individual bowls, serve the meat sauce, cucumbers, scallions, and cilantro so that each eater can customize their noodles. For extra spice, spoon chile paste or oil on top.

1 1-pound package **dried or fresh Shanghai-style noodles**

3 tablespoons **Asian sesame oil**

1 tablespoon **vegetable oil**

3 **garlic cloves**, minced

1½ pounds **ground pork**

6 1½-inch squares **pressed bean curd**

6 ounces fresh **shiitake mushrooms** (about 8 large mushrooms), cut into small dice

1 cup **mung bean sprouts**, roots discarded

3 tablespoons *zha jiang* **soybean paste**

3 tablespoons **hoisin sauce**

3 tablespoons **soy sauce**

2 **Persian cucumbers**, unpeeled, halved crosswise and thinly julienned

4 **scallions** (green and white parts), halved crosswise and julienned

½ cup chopped fresh **cilantro leaves and stems**

Chili paste or **chili oil** (optional)

CURRYING FLAVOR

Curries tell a fascinating story of the spice trade, when spices like cardamom, ginger, and turmeric were traded between Asia, northeast Africa, and Europe. The spice trade was once the world's largest industry, one that built and destroyed empires and led to the discovery of new lands. Because curries of many national styles became popular in lands far from their Asian origins thanks to the Spice Road, I consider them to be one of the earliest global dishes.

Whether wet or dry, vegetarian or meaty, mild or fiery, quickly assembled or long-simmered, curries are now the backbone of home cooking in many countries. I like to think of them as the rainbow of cuisines, a flavorful blend of spices like coriander, cumin, and turmeric and a dish that takes on colorful characteristics unique to each culture—from Thailand to India, China to Japan. My favorite Southeast Asian curries are a melting pot of cuisines including Indian, Spanish, Chinese, and French. And if that sounds like a hodgepodge of cultures, that's precisely the point. My brother once went to Singapore's Little India, and as an experiment bought one of each spice within a collection and made a curry using equal amounts of each of the twenty he bought. The result was surprisingly delicious, with each new bite offering more flavor nuances than the previous.

However, if there's one cuisine that seems inseparable from curry, it's Indian. The curry leaf comes from curry trees indigenous to India and neighboring Sri Lanka. Despite the name of the dish, however, the curry leaf is not always essential to making "curry," which comes from the Tamil word *kari*, which means sauce. By the same token, chiles and curries don't necessarily go hand in hand. Even though some fire alarm–inducing recipes such as Indian vindaloo and Thai jungle curry contain copious amounts of chiles, many Southeast Asian curries (like those from Vietnam or Cambodia) are actually quite mild.

INDIAN-SPICED TOMATO SOUP

SERVES 6

Like my Asian Gazpacho (page 137), this soup is inspired by Silicon Valley—its bounty of beautiful summer tomatoes coupled with the wave of immigrants, many from India, who have helped fuel the tech boom. While the rich flavors of Indian curries and other stick-to-the-ribs dishes have become mainstream in the American diet, more elegant and refined flavors of Indian cuisine—which often make abundant use of South Asian spices like the coriander in this recipe—are finding their way into our Indian food vernacular.

10 ripe medium **tomatoes** (about 4 pounds), or 2 28-ounce cans **whole peeled tomatoes**, including the juices

1 tablespoon **vegetable oil**

1 medium **yellow onion**, chopped

4 **garlic cloves**, crushed

1 **bay leaf**

2 tablespoons chopped fresh **cilantro**, plus whole leaves for garnish

1 tablespoon ground **coriander**

¼ cup **heavy cream**

4 tablespoons (½ stick) **unsalted butter**

Salt and freshly **ground white pepper**, to taste

If you are using fresh tomatoes, bring a large pot of salted water to a boil. Add the tomatoes, immediately turn off the heat, and let them sit for about 3 minutes, until the skin starts to crack and separate from the fruit. Drain the tomatoes in a colander and rinse them under cold running water. Peel off the skins, and transfer the tomatoes to a large bowl, reserving the juices.

Heat the vegetable oil in the empty pot over medium heat, add the onion and garlic, and cook for 2 minutes, until the onions start to soften. Add the bay leaf, cilantro, and coriander and cook for 2 minutes. Remove the pot from the heat and discard the bay leaf. Allow to cool slightly.

Put the onion mixture in a blender, add half of the tomatoes (or one of the cans of tomatoes with their juices), and puree until smooth. Pour the puree back into the pot, and puree the remaining tomatoes in the blender. Add the puree to the pot and heat thoroughly until warm. Add the cream and butter, and season with salt and white pepper to taste. Cook for 2 to 3 more minutes to melt the butter and meld the flavors. Don't overcook, or the fresh taste of the tomatoes may be lost. Serve with whole cilantro leaves for garnish.

Serve this soup alongside blocks of grilled paneer cheese (a fresh, non-fermented cheese common to South Asian cuisine) for a new take on the grilled-cheese-and-tomato-soup combo.

CURRY IN A HURRY

SERVES 4 TO 6

New York City taxi drivers, many of whom hail from countries where curries are staples—be it Pakistan, India, Trinidad, or Jamaica—are notorious for their love of curry, whose lingering aroma perfumes many a taxicab. When it comes to curry joints, New York City is indeed the city that never sleeps: at Mott Corner restaurant in Chinatown and diners in Jackson Heights, you will find queues of off-duty taxis parked out front and their drivers inside, gobbling down curry between shifts. Some people think that curry has to be slow-simmered for hours but that's a myth. Here's my go-to for a quick curry. Try it the next time you're in a hurry to get good food to the table.

Heat the vegetable oil in a large skillet over medium-high heat. Add the onion, ginger, and garlic and cook, stirring often, for 3 to 4 minutes, until the onions start to turn translucent. Add the chicken and cook, stirring occasionally, until it starts to brown, 4 to 5 minutes.

Add the curry paste, apple cider vinegar, and garam masala and stir well, cooking for 2 to 3 minutes, until the curry paste smells fragrant. Then add the tomatoes, breaking them up with a wooden spoon, bring the liquid to a boil, and reduce the heat. Simmer gently for 20 to 25 minutes, until the sauce has thickened and the chicken is cooked through. Taste, and add kosher salt if needed. Sprinkle the cilantro over the curry, and serve with steamed rice on the side.

2 tablespoons **vegetable oil**

1 large **yellow onion**, diced

1 2-inch knob fresh **ginger**, minced

3 **garlic cloves**, minced

1½ pounds boneless, skinless **chicken thighs**, cut into large pieces

½ cup mild **yellow Indian curry paste**

⅓ cup **apple cider vinegar**

2 teaspoons **garam masala**

1 28-ounce can **whole tomatoes**, drained

Kosher salt, to taste

½ cup chopped fresh **cilantro leaves**

Perfect Steamed Rice (page 145), for serving

THAI GREEN CURRY COCONUT MUSSELS

SERVES 4

Green curry, made with green chiles and coconut milk, is spicier than Thai red or yellow curries. With a supply of Thai green curry paste on hand, this Asian version of a traditional French steamed mussel dish can be made in under 10 minutes. Instead of a baguette to soak up the juices from the mussels, try serving steamed white rice; long-grain jasmine rice works perfectly and doesn't become overly congealed in the liquid.

Chop the garlic and ginger together until very finely minced, pressing with the flat of the knife blade to turn the mixture into almost a paste.

Melt the butter in a large pot over medium heat. Add the garlic-ginger paste and stir until fragrant, about 30 seconds. Add the shallots and lemongrass and cook for 1 to 2 minutes, until the shallots start to soften. Stir in the coconut milk, fish sauce, and curry paste, raise the heat to high, and bring the mixture to a boil. Add the mussels and cover the pot. Cook for 4 to 5 minutes, until the mussels are fully opened.

Remove the pot from the heat and discard any mussels that haven't opened. Stir in the basil, cilantro, and lime juice, tossing to coat the mussels thoroughly in the sauce. Serve at once, with hot jasmine rice to soak up the sauce.

1 1-inch knob fresh **ginger**

2 **garlic cloves**

3 tablespoons **unsalted butter**

2 **shallots**, finely minced

3 **lemongrass stalks**, trimmed and finely chopped

1 15-ounce can **coconut milk**

3 tablespoons **fish sauce**

2 tablespoons **Thai green curry paste**

3 pounds **mussels**, scrubbed and debearded

¼ cup chopped fresh **basil**

¼ cup chopped fresh **cilantro leaves**

Juice of 2 **limes**

Hot steamed jasmine rice, for serving

SPICY FISH STEW

Shui Zhu Yu

SERVES 6

The name of this dish means "water-boiled fish," but most restaurant versions call for poaching the fish in hot, spicy oil. This home-style rendition uses significantly less oil and stays true to a quick-cooking poached fish stew. It has an intensely aromatic and flavorful broth thanks to the signature flavor of the Sichuanese peppercorns: a fragrant, citrus-like taste with a tingly finish that your lips and tongue will remember for hours afterward. Despite its notoriety for spicy cuisine, Sichuanese food is actually all about balance—numbing peppercorns tempered with pungent preserved vegetables and salty-sweet bean pastes. I always turn to this satisfying stew to take advantage of any number of fish I might find at the market—from catfish to cod—and, of course, to give me an excuse to eat even more peppercorns.

Place the mushrooms in a bowl, add warm water to cover, and let soak for about 30 minutes, until rehydrated.

Meanwhile, cut the fish fillets into thin slices. In a large bowl, combine the fish slices with the rice wine, cornstarch, and kosher salt. Set aside and let marinate for at least 15 minutes.

Heat 2 tablespoons of the vegetable oil in a large wok over high heat. Add the star anise, garlic, ginger, and scallion whites and stir-fry until fragrant, about 1 minute. Add 1 teaspoon of the peppercorns and 5 of the dried chiles, and stir-fry for another minute. Add the broad bean paste and continue to stir-fry for another minute.

Add the celery, napa cabbage, and drained shiitake mushrooms to the wok. Add 2 cups of water, or enough to cover, and simmer for about 30 minutes, until the vegetables are tender.

6 large **dried shiitake mushrooms**

1½ pounds fresh **white fish fillets** (such as red snapper)

2 tablespoons **rice wine**

2 tablespoons **cornstarch**

1 tablespoon **kosher salt**

4 tablespoons **vegetable oil**

2 **star anise pods**

5 **garlic cloves**, smashed

1 2-inch knob fresh **ginger**, sliced

2 **scallions**, green and white parts chopped separately

2 teaspoons **Sichuanese peppercorns**

10 **dried red chiles**

2 tablespoons **spicy broad bean paste** (*doubanjiang*)

1 cup chopped **Chinese celery or standard celery**

½ medium head **napa cabbage**, quartered lengthwise and then cut into 2-inch pieces

Perfect Steamed Rice (page 145), for serving

Remove the fish fillets from their marinade and add them to the wok; cook until the fish is just opaque, about 2 minutes. Remove the wok from the heat and transfer the contents to a serving dish.

In a small skillet, heat the remaining 2 tablespoons vegetable oil over medium-high heat. Add the remaining 1 teaspoon peppercorns and 5 chiles, and stir-fry for about a minute, until fragrant (the amount of spice can be adjusted to your liking).

Just before serving, pour the hot oil over the stew and garnish with the chopped scallion greens. Serve over hot rice.

ASIAN MASH-UPS

KIMCHI TACOS
Page 117

Fusion cooking may be the best thing that's happened to Asian cuisine. When cultures collide, chefs collaborate, and when chefs collaborate, our culinary culture evolves. Fusion cuisine today is nothing like the fusion movement of the 1990s, which introduced us to ill-conceived dishes—like mashed potatoes with wasabi—that haphazardly fused random ingredients and subsequently gave the term a bad rep. Since then, chefs have been fighting off the stigma of "Asian fusion cuisine."

For some reason, we've developed the misconception that good Asian food must be authentic. But really, what's more authentic than dishes that are created from the coming together of cultures, ingredients, and cooking techniques? So much innovation in the Asian food world is a result of chefs who cross boundaries—like American chef Andy Ricker, who turned a backpacking adventure in Thailand into a mission to re-create northern Thai cuisine in Portland, Oregon, or the Jewish New Yorker, chef Ivan Orkin, who boldly thought to melt schmaltz in ramen.

Many "authentic" (and beloved) fusion foods are rooted in history. *Banh mi* would not have been birthed were it not for the French colonization of Vietnam. Tempura, the Japanese deep-fried specialty, was brought by Portuguese missionaries to Japan. And more recently, Asian ingredients have fused with Western classics like pastrami.

All of the recipes in this chapter are the products of cultural collaboration—dishes created over time, thanks to migration, adaptation, and innovation. There's Peru's popular *lomo saltado* (page 133), a cousin to the classic Chinese stir-fry, created by immigrants. Or Chicken *Tikka Masala* (page 135), an "authentic" Indian dish created to suit the British appetite for milder, creamier, tomato-based curries. If the future of cuisine looks anything like the human face of the future, then it will be even more interwoven—after all, food is nothing if not a living, breathing craft that evolves with our own taste buds.

KIMCHI TACOS

MAKES 8 TACOS, SERVES 4

Born out of Los Angeles' Koreatown, kimchi tacos—which substitute the fiery flavors of kimchi for the traditional salsa—epitomize the city's hipster food scene. L.A. chef Roy Choi popped up with his Kogi taco truck in 2008, and wherever the truck went, fans would follow, stalking its whereabouts on Twitter and flocking to the truck like teenage groupies running after Jon Bon Jovi's limo in the '80s. Roy was right to bring his fusion tacos to the neighborhood; L.A. is home to the largest concentration of Koreans outside of Asia, but even more Hispanics live in Koreatown than Koreans! So you see, tortillas and kimchi were destined to become good friends. What could be more authentically fusion?

In a small bowl, make the taco sauce by combining the sugar, *gochujang*, soy sauce, sesame oil, and rice vinegar. Stir well and set aside.

Heat a charcoal or gas grill and oil the grate. Sear the beef to medium-rare, about 2 minutes on each side; then let it rest for 5 minutes. Slice the meat diagonally across the grain into ½-inch-thick pieces.

Heat the tortillas by wrapping them in a clean damp towel and microwaving them for 30 seconds, or by giving them a quick turn on the grill, about 30 seconds per side.

Divide the meat pieces among the warmed tortillas. To serve, top each one with kimchi, taco sauce, chopped cilantro, and a squeeze of lime.

2 tablespoons **sugar**

¼ cup *gochujang* **chili paste**

¼ cup **soy sauce**

1 tablespoon **Asian sesame oil**

2 teaspoons **rice vinegar**

Vegetable oil, for the grate

1 pound **beef short ribs**, cut LA Galbi–style, deboned, and marinated (see page 132 for explanation and marinade)

8 **corn tortillas**

2 cups **kimchi** (see page 45)

Chopped fresh **cilantro leaves**, for serving

Lime wedges, for serving

JEWISH PASTRAMI EGG ROLLS

MAKES 10 EGG ROLLS

It wasn't until I moved to New York City for college that I learned how much affinity the Jewish population there has for Chinese food. In joining my new Jewish friends for Sunday dinners, I was surprised that we'd usually end up having Chinese food, some of which was even kosher! Since then, I've learned a great deal about Chinese food from my friend Ed Schoenfeld, the New York restaurateur behind Red Farm and self-described Chinese food expert who popularized this egg roll with pastrami, which tastes like the Chinese specialty *la rou* but is much easier to find and is quintessentially New York.

Heat the vegetable oil in a skillet over medium heat. Add the onion and cook for 4 to 5 minutes, until translucent. Scrape the onions into a medium bowl, add the pastrami strips, sauerkraut, mustard, and mayonnaise and toss to mix well.

For each egg roll, lay a wrapper on a clean work surface with one point facing you, forming a diamond shape. Put a heaping tablespoon of the filling in the center and fold the bottom point up, just over the filling. Fold the two side points over the center, and then dab a little water on the top point. Roll upward to seal the top. Repeat with the remaining wrappers and filling. Lay the egg rolls on a baking sheet, spacing them so they do not touch. Line a serving platter with paper towels and set it near the stove.

Pour vegetable oil into a large heavy-bottomed saucepan to a depth of 1½ inches. Heat the oil over medium heat until it measures 350°F on a deep-frying thermometer. Working in batches, fry the egg rolls for 2 to 3 minutes, until the outside of the wrapper is golden brown and slightly blistered. As they are done, transfer the cooked egg rolls to the platter. Serve at once, with extra mustard on the side.

1 tablespoon **vegetable oil**, plus more for frying the egg rolls

1 small **yellow onion**, diced

¼ pound **lean pastrami**, cut into thin strips

1½ cups **prepared sauerkraut**, well drained

2 tablespoons **brown mustard**, plus more for serving

2 tablespoons **mayonnaise**

10 **egg roll wrappers** (available by the package in the frozen food section of Asian groceries), thawed

★ ★
NOTE

Sticky rice cakes are popular across Asian cultures (called *nian gao* in Chinese, *mochi* in Japanese, and *tteok* in Korean). They can be found packaged and pre-sliced in the frozen food section of Asian groceries.

U.S. ARMY STEW

Budae Jjigae
SERVES 4

Along with kimchi, Spam (yes, *Spam*) and hot dogs make their way into this everything-but-the-kitchen-sink stew. *Budae jjigae* (which translates as "army stew") has its origins in the rations of luncheon meat that American GIs received during the Korean War. With the addition of instant ramen and mozzarella cheese, which were also introduced to Korea, this stew has become a late-night dish or hangover restorative throughout South Korea, especially at *pochas*, which are tented street food stalls. I was introduced to this dish in Manhattan's Koreatown, a one-block strip of 32nd Street that feels like Seoul, with its vertical buildings filled with karaoke bars, massage parlors, and restaurants. Pocha 32 is one such joint, and as the evening (or morning) wears on, you'll find watermelon *soju* (see page 181) and a bubbling-hot cauldron of *budae jjigae* on every table. This stew is quite delicious (and tastes even better after a couple of shots of *soju*!).

In a large stockpot, heat the vegetable oil over medium heat. Add the garlic and onion and sauté until just softened, about 2 minutes. Stir in the *gochujang* to your preferred level of spiciness. Add 2 cups of water and bring to a boil. Stir in the fish sauce, rice wine, scallions, zucchini, mushrooms, kimchi, Spam, and hot dogs. Cook at a low boil for about 5 minutes, until the vegetables have softened.

Add the rice cakes and ramen noodles and cook for 2 to 3 minutes, until both are cooked through. Nestle the tofu chunks into the stew, and top with the mozzarella cheese. Cover the pot and cook for another 2 minutes, or until the cheese has melted.

Top with the watercress if desired, and serve table-side with hot rice and a large ladle.

2 tablespoons **vegetable oil**

4 **garlic cloves**, minced

½ medium **onion**, chopped

Up to 4 tablespoons *gochujang* **chili paste**

2 tablespoons **fish sauce**

2 tablespoons **rice wine** (mirin or *mijiu*)

1 bunch **scallions** (green and white parts), chopped

1 medium **zucchini**, chopped

5 to 6 **white mushrooms** (caps and stems), quartered

1 cup **kimchi** (see page 45)

½ can **Spam**, chopped

2 **hot dogs**, sliced into ½-inch rounds

½ cup **frozen sticky rice cake**, thawed (see Note)

1 package **instant ramen noodles**, seasoning packet discarded

½ pound **firm tofu**, cut into 1-inch cubes

½ cup **shredded mozzarella cheese**

1 bunch fresh **watercress**, chopped (optional)

Perfect Steamed Rice (page 145), for serving

MACANESE AFRICAN CHICKEN

SERVES 4

This "African" chicken is not African, but rather a Macanese classic blended with Chinese and Spanish spices. Thanks to Macau's status as a former Portuguese colony, its cuisine is made up of an amalgamation of ingredients that the Portuguese sailors brought with them when they established their first settlement in the 1500s, and now the cuisine incorporates influences from Europe, Africa, India, Malaysia, Latin America, and, of course, China. The island—along with Hong Kong—was ceded to China in 1999, and today Macau is the world's most profitable gambling destination, welcoming the Chinese (and their propensity for gambling) by the boatload. With gambling and casino culture comes a lively appetite for entertainment and dining, so many of the world's most famous chefs have recently made their way there.

PREPARE THE CHICKEN: In a large bowl, mix together the garlic, shallots, paprika, kosher salt, and bay leaves. Add the chicken and rub the marinade all over it. Cover the bowl with plastic wrap and marinate in the refrigerator for at least 1 hour or as long as overnight.

MAKE THE SAUCE: Heat the olive oil in a large saucepan over medium heat. Add the shallots and garlic, and cook until softened, about 3 minutes. Add the paprika, coconut milk, chicken broth, and peanut butter and simmer over low heat until blended, about 10 minutes. Set aside.

Preheat the oven to 400°F. In a large heavy skillet, heat the remaining 2 tablespoons olive oil. Remove the chicken from the marinade and sauté until it is browned on all sides, about 10 minutes. Transfer the chicken to a baking dish and spoon the sauce evenly over it. Bake for about 30 minutes, until bubbly. Serve with steamed rice alongside.

FOR THE CHICKEN:

1 tablespoon minced **garlic**

2 tablespoons minced **shallots**

1 teaspoon **hot paprika**

1 tablespoon **kosher salt**

2 **bay leaves**, crumbled

1 large **chicken** (approximately 4 pounds), quartered

2 tablespoons **olive oil**

FOR THE SAUCE:

2 tablespoons **olive oil**

1 cup chopped **shallots**

8 **garlic cloves**, chopped

1 teaspoon **hot paprika**

1 16-ounce can **coconut milk**

½ cup **chicken broth**

¼ cup **smooth peanut butter**

Perfect Steamed Rice (page 145), for serving

WHEN IN ROME, EAT CHINESE

"The Chinese are like cockroaches," my dad would say with a grin. "They find their way into every corner of the world and adapt." This certainly is true when it comes to Chinese food. It seems that no matter where you go, there you are—in a cheap and cheerful Chinese restaurant. Whether you're in Tijuana or Juneau, you will find a Chinese family reliably serving up egg rolls and egg drop soup in a restaurant invariably crowned with an auspicious-sounding name such as Grand Harmony, Jade Pavilion, or Joy Palace and marked by a lucky cat waving at you from behind the window. These menus are remarkably universal, as if there were an underground global kitchen from which you can dig your way to China. But what I take pleasure in is how each restaurant adapts that universal menu to satisfy local palates, for example the way the Peruvian-Chinese stir-fry *lomo saltado* (page 133) is served with both potatoes and rice.

I grew up in a household that ate exclusively Chinese food. Today much of the joy I experience in traveling is in sampling local foods, and thankfully even my dad has come to broaden his food horizon. But back then, after a week of eating foreign foods on our family trips abroad, a craving for comforting, familiar flavors would settle in. We'd spend a day at the Louvre or at the Roman Coliseum and then, like clockwork, my dad would guide us to the nearest dumpy Chinese restaurant. I would joke that the motto of "When in Rome, do as the Romans do" did not apply to the Changs as we made our way past the charming trattorias, with their irresistible thin-crust pizzas and freshly made pastas, to some nondescript Chinese restaurant marked by neon lights outside and iridescent lighting inside. But no matter—that's where we'd find soy sauce and steamed rice, which tasted better to my dad's homesick Chinese palate than any combination of pasta and truffles.

So you can imagine our surprise when, on that trip to Italy with my dad, we ended up having an exceptional home-style Chinese meal in the middle of Rome. It turned out that the chef and owner was also from Wenzhou, the city to the south of Shanghai where my dad was born. Ironically, that was the most memorable moment of our family vacation: to travel halfway around the world to Piazza Navona only to find food from our homeland.

ROMAN-CHINESE OXTAIL STEW

SERVES 6

Italian and Chinese home cooking share many similarities: While it may not be obvious, both cultures have a love of offal, such as tripe and liver, and so this oxtail-based dish perfectly fuses the two traditions on one plate. I simmer the oxtails in a combination of classic Italian ragù ingredients like red wine and tomatoes and Chinese flavors like soy sauce and bean paste. I like to serve this saucy dish over thin spaghetti, or a nice crusty ciabatta would also work well for sopping up the extra sauce.

Bring a large pot of salted water to a boil. Add the oxtail pieces and simmer for about 15 minutes. Drain the oxtail pieces and rinse them under cold running water. Rinse out the pot and set aside.

Heat the olive oil in a large frying pan or wok over medium-high heat. When the oil is sizzling, add the onion and garlic and stir-fry for 1 minute. Then add the oxtail and stir-fry until they are lightly browned, 5 minutes. Stir in the star anise, soy sauce, red wine, sugar, bean paste, and pepper and simmer for 2 minutes.

Transfer the contents of the pan to the empty pot. Add the tomatoes and 1 cup of the chicken broth. Bring the mixture to a boil; then reduce the heat to a simmer and skim off any excess fat or oil. Cover the pot and simmer, skimming occasionally, for about 2½ hours, until the oxtail meat is nearly falling off the bones.

Add the celery, carrots, potatoes, and scallions. If the mixture is too thick to stir, add another cup of broth. Cover the pot and simmer for 30 minutes, or until the vegetables are tender.

If using, divide the noodles among 6 dishes. Pile 1 or 2 oxtail pieces in each dish, and ladle the vegetables and broth on top.

3 pounds **beef oxtail pieces**, cut into about 1½-inch slices (ask your butcher to do this for you)

2 tablespoons **olive oil**

1 large **yellow onion**, chopped

8 **garlic cloves**, smashed

6 **star anise pods**

½ cup **soy sauce**

½ cup **fruity red wine**

2 tablespoons **sugar** (preferably Chinese rock sugar)

3 tablespoons **broad bean paste** (*doubanjiang*)

1 teaspoon freshly **ground black pepper**

1 28-ounce can **whole tomatoes**, drained and coarsely chopped

1 to 2 cups **chicken broth**

3 **celery stalks**, cut into 1-inch pieces

3 large **carrots**, cut into 1-inch pieces

2 medium **potatoes**, such as Yukon Golds, peeled and cut into eighths

4 **scallions** (green and white parts), chopped

1 pound **cooked thin spaghetti**, or **crusty ciabatta bread**, for serving

★ ★
NOTE
This recipe yields plenty—enough
for seconds! Leftovers will keep in
the freezer for up to 2 months. Thaw
in the fridge before reheating on the
stovetop.

ABC BEEF WITH BROCCOLI

SERVES 6

I consider Chinese American (also known by the acronym ABC, or American-Born Chinese) cuisine to be a regional specialty—like Shanghainese, Cantonese, or Sichuanese—inspired by regional ingredients and palates. Ironically, ABC expats living in China are now opening restaurants serving the Chinese American food that they grew up with back in the U.S. There are nearly 41,000 Chinese take-out restaurants in the United States—that's three times the number of McDonalds! In most of these restaurants, you'll find a Westernized Chinese menu that's takeout-friendly and usually caters to an old-school American palate, with a preference for sweeter, milder flavors and crunchy fried foods. This home-style recipe for beef with broccoli, however, is lighter in oil and salt than the heavier brown sauce version you typically get in Chinese fast-food joints.

FOR THE BEEF AND VEGETABLES:

1 tablespoon **soy sauce**

2 teaspoons **rice wine**

1 teaspoon **Asian sesame oil**

2 tablespoons **cornstarch**

¼ teaspoon **ground white pepper**

1 pound **boneless beef round steak**, cut into thin strips

1 head **broccoli**, broken into florets

1 teaspoon **sesame seeds**

2 tablespoons **vegetable oil**

1 2-inch knob fresh **ginger**, minced

2 **garlic cloves**, minced

PREPARE THE BEEF AND VEGETABLES: Combine the soy sauce, rice wine, sesame oil, cornstarch, and white pepper in a medium bowl. Add the beef strips and toss to coat. Allow to marinate at room temperature for at least 10 minutes and as long as 30 minutes.

While the meat marinates, bring a medium saucepan of lightly salted water to a boil. When the water is boiling, add the broccoli florets and cook for 1 minute, until they are bright green. Drain and rinse well under cold running water to stop the cooking.

Heat a wok over high heat and add the sesame seeds. Cook, tossing the wok, for 30 seconds to 1 minute, until the sesame seeds are fragrant and lightly browned. Immediately turn them into a medium bowl and set aside.

In the same wok, heat the vegetable oil over medium-high heat. Add half the marinated beef, removed from the marinade, plus all the ginger and garlic, and stir-fry for 2 minutes, until the beef is lightly browned. Transfer the beef and aromatics to the bowl containing the sesame seeds, and repeat with the remaining beef (no need to add more oil). When the second batch is cooked, return the first batch, with the toasted sesame seeds, to the wok. Add the blanched broccoli and toss to combine and heat through.

MAKE THE SAUCE: Combine the soy sauce, oyster sauce, sesame oil, and red chile flakes, if using, in a small saucepan. Cook, stirring, for 3 to 4 minutes, until the sauce is thick. Add the sauce to the beef and broccoli, and quickly stir-fry to combine. Serve immediately, with hot steamed rice on the side.

FOR THE SAUCE:

2 tablespoons **soy sauce**

2 tablespoons **oyster sauce**

½ teaspoon **Asian sesame oil**

¼ teaspoon crushed **red chile flakes** (optional)

Perfect Steamed Rice (page 145), for serving

VIETNAMESE *BANH MI*

SERVES 6

Banh mi, which translates simply as "bread," is a packed hoagie-style sandwich that is a product of French colonialism in Indochina. French ingredients like fresh baguettes and mayonnaise are combined with Vietnamese ingredients such as cilantro, fish sauce, and pickled carrots to create this everyday fusion sandwich. Today in the United States, especially in large Vietnamese communities like those in Houston or the San Francisco Bay Area, *banh mi* shops are seemingly everywhere. There the French baguette dough is cut with rice flour to create a crispier crust and an overall lighter bread, a perfect container for savory meat fillings balanced by a fresh, crunchy, sweet-sour pickled vegetable slaw.

PREPARE THE MEAT: Combine the shallot, garlic, ginger, lemongrass, brown sugar, soy sauce, fish sauce, and vegetable oil in a food processor. Pulse to chop up the aromatics; then let the machine run for 1 to 2 minutes, until you have a smooth paste. Put the pork tenderloin in a self-seal plastic bag and add the spice paste. Seal the bag and massage the paste onto the pork, turning it to coat it completely. Let the meat marinate at room temperature for 1 hour, or in the refrigerator for 2 to 24 hours.

MEANWHILE, MAKE THE SLAW: Toss the carrot and daikon together in a medium heatproof bowl. Combine the vinegar, granulated sugar, kosher salt, and ½ cup of water in a small saucepan and bring to a boil over high heat. Pour the mixture over the carrot and daikon. Cover the bowl, and let the slaw sit for 1 hour at room temperature or in the refrigerator for up to 24 hours. Before serving, drain the slaw, discarding the liquid. When you are ready to cook, preheat the oven to 400°F.

FOR THE MEAT:

1 **shallot**, coarsely chopped

3 **garlic cloves**

1 1-inch knob fresh **ginger**, coarsely chopped

1 **lemongrass stalk**, trimmed and cut into 1-inch pieces

1 teaspoon **dark brown sugar**

1 tablespoon **dark soy sauce**

1½ tablespoons **fish sauce**

1 tablespoon **vegetable oil**

1½ pounds **pork tenderloin**

FOR THE SLAW:

1 large **carrot**, shredded

1 medium **daikon**, shredded

¼ cup **distilled white vinegar**

1 tablespoon **granulated sugar**

1 teaspoon **kosher salt**

COOK THE MEAT: Put the marinated pork in a small roasting pan or cast-iron skillet. Roast for 12 to 15 minutes, until the center reads 145°F on an instant-read thermometer. Remove the pork from the oven, cover it loosely with foil, and let it rest for at least 5 minutes before slicing.

ASSEMBLE THE SANDWICHES: Thinly slice the pork and halve the baguette rolls or pieces horizontally. Spread mayonnaise on each side of the bread, and top one side with pork, slaw, cilantro, and cucumber. Cover the toppings with the other side of the bread. Serve with Sriracha on the side.

FOR THE SANDWICHES:

6 large, **crusty baguette rolls** (or 3 large baguettes cut into 10-inch lengths)

¾ cup **mayonnaise**

¾ cup fresh **cilantro sprigs**

½ large **seedless cucumber**, thinly sliced lengthwise

Sriracha, for serving

ASIAN MASH-UPS

GRILLED KOREAN
SHORT RIBS

Page 132

GRILLED KOREAN SHORT RIBS

LA Galbi

SERVES 6

When it comes to Korean food, many of us think of barbecue and the fun built-in tabletop grills at Korean restaurants. Korean barbecues are easy to master at home, and they are a great way to experiment with different cuts of meat on the grill. The "LA Galbi" cut—which means thinly sliced across the bone (about a quarter-inch thick)—originated with Korean immigrants living in Los Angeles (though the LA stands for lateral, not Los Angeles!). The added pear really tenderizes the meat and adds a honey glaze.

In a blender, combine the onion, garlic cloves, ginger, sugar, black pepper, soy sauce, pear, and mirin and puree until smooth.

Put the meat in a large self-seal plastic bag. Pour the puree into the bag and massage the puree into the meat. Seal tightly and refrigerate overnight.

On a charcoal grill or a tableside grill, remove the ribs from the marinade and cook for about 5 minutes, turning them over halfway through, for medium doneness. Use kitchen shears to cut the meat apart into bite-size pieces, discarding the bones.

To serve, smear some *gochujang* paste on each lettuce leaf, add some meat, and top with some sliced garlic, sliced jalapeño, perilla leaves, and scallions. Wrap the lettuce around the contents, and serve with hot steamed rice.

★★ TIP Save some of the grilled short rib meat for Kimchi Tacos (page 117).

1 medium **yellow onion**, quartered

6 to 8 **garlic cloves**, plus 2 to 3 sliced cloves for serving

1 1-inch knob fresh **ginger**, smashed

½ cup **sugar**

1 teaspoon freshly **ground black pepper**

½ cup **soy sauce**

1 medium **pear**, quartered (preferably a Korean "nashi" pear, commonly known as an Asian pear)

½ cup **mirin or other rice-based wine**

3 pounds **beef short ribs**, cut LA Galbi–style (see headnote)

Gochujang **chili paste**, for serving

2 heads **red-leaf or romaine lettuce**, torn into palm-size pieces

1 medium **jalapeño pepper**, sliced

Fresh perilla or mint leaves, for serving

3 **scallions** (green and white parts), thinly sliced

Perfect Steamed Rice (page 145), for serving

PERUVIAN STIR-FRIED BEEF WITH TOMATOES

Lomo Saltado

SERVES 4

Lomo saltado, a Chinese-style stir-fry that's served with both potatoes and rice, is perhaps Peru's most famous dish. The Chinese influence in Peru came in a similar way as it did to the West Coast in the United States; just as Chinese men immigrated to California to build the railroads and work in the mining camps, masses of Chinese came to Peru during the commercial agriculture boom on Peru's coast. Peruvian Chinese food is called *chifa*, which is a Latinization of the Chinese word *chifan*, which simply means "to eat." Even though the origins of *saltados*, or stir-fries, are Chinese, the resulting *criollo* cuisine is actually considered the national cuisine of Peru, and this dish is the best expression of that tradition.

Heat the vegetable oil in a large wok over medium-high heat. Add the steak strips, season them with salt and pepper, and stir-fry until browned on both sides, about 5 minutes. Transfer the meat to a plate and set aside.

Add the red onion, tomatoes, and garlic to the same wok, season the vegetables with salt and pepper, and stir-fry until the tomatoes and onions are soft, about 5 minutes.

Return the beef to the wok, and pour the soy sauce and red wine vinegar over the top. Stir-fry for about 2 minutes, seasoning with additional salt and pepper if needed, until the ingredients are well combined. Serve family-style, with rice and fried potatoes alongside.

1 tablespoon **vegetable oil**

1½ pounds **rib-eye steak**, sliced into 1-inch-wide strips

Salt and freshly **ground black pepper**, to taste

1 large **red onion**, quartered and thinly sliced

2 large **tomatoes**, coarsely chopped

1 **garlic clove**, minced

1 tablespoon **soy sauce**

1 tablespoon **red wine vinegar**

Perfect Steamed Rice (page 145), for serving

Hot French fries or other fried potatoes, for serving

CHICKEN *TIKKA MASALA*

SERVES 6

Widely served in Indian restaurants across the United Kingdom and North America, this fragrant tomato and cream–based curry dish is so popular that British foreign secretary Robin Cook declared it to be a British national dish—not just because of its popularity, but because "it is a perfect illustration of the way Britain absorbs and adapts external influences." While the exact origins of chicken *tikka masala* are unclear, it is commonly acknowledged that the dish resulted from adapting a traditional South Asian tandoori dish (chicken *tikka*) by adding a tomato and cream sauce to cater to the British love for gravy and spiced meat.

PREPARE THE CHICKEN: Place the chicken in a large self-seal plastic bag. In a small bowl, combine the yogurt, lemon juice, ginger, garlic, garam masala, cumin, paprika, and kosher salt, then add it to the plastic bag. Seal the bag well and turn it to combine the ingredients, massaging the marinade into the chicken. Marinate for at least 1 hour at room temperature, or refrigerate and marinate for up to 24 hours.

MAKE THE SAUCE: Heat the vegetable oil in a large skillet over medium-high heat. Add the onion, ginger, and garlic. Cook, stirring occasionally, for 6 to 8 minutes, until the onions have softened and begun to turn lightly golden. In a small bowl, combine the cinnamon, turmeric, cayenne, cardamom, and cloves and mix together. Add the mixed spices to the skillet, stirring, for 1 to 2 minutes, until the spices are fragrant.

Pour the tomatoes, with their juices, and 1 cup of water into the skillet. Stir to combine, and bring the mixture to a boil. Then reduce the heat to medium and simmer gently until the sauce has thickened, 30 minutes.

recipe continues

FOR THE CHICKEN:

6 boneless, skinless **chicken thighs**, chopped into 2-inch pieces

1 cup **full-fat plain yogurt**

⅓ cup fresh **lemon juice**

1 1-inch knob fresh **ginger**, minced

3 **garlic cloves**, minced

4 teaspoons **garam masala**

1 tablespoon ground **cumin**

2 teaspoons **sweet paprika**

1 teaspoon **kosher salt**

FOR THE SAUCE:

2 tablespoons **vegetable oil**

1 large **yellow onion**, chopped

1 2-inch knob fresh **ginger**, minced

8 **garlic cloves**, minced

1 teaspoon ground **cinnamon**

1 teaspoon ground **turmeric**

½ teaspoon ground **cayenne pepper**

¼ teaspoon ground **cardamom**

¼ teaspoon ground **cloves**

1 28-ounce can **diced tomatoes**, with juices

¼ cup **heavy cream** or **full-fat Greek yogurt**

1 tablespoon **garam masala**

Chopped fresh **cilantro leaves**, for serving

Hot steamed basmati rice, for serving

While the sauce simmers, heat the broiler on the highest setting for 10 minutes, and line a baking sheet with aluminum foil.

Lift the chicken pieces out of the bag, reserving the marinade, and thread them onto metal skewers, being sure not to crowd the pieces too closely. Place the skewers on the lined baking sheet. (You can skip the skewers if you prefer, but the chicken will be more tender and cook more evenly with the hot skewer carrying heat through the center of each piece.) Stir the reserved marinade into the simmering sauce.

Broil the chicken for 8 minutes. Then turn the skewers over and broil for another 6 to 8 minutes, until the meat is well browned, even a little dark around the edges. Remove the chicken from the skewers.

Using a stick blender, puree the sauce with the heavy cream until smooth (or puree the sauce and cream together, in batches, in a standing blender, and then return the pureed sauce to the skillet). Stir in the garam masala, and add the chicken. Cook, stirring, for 3 to 4 minutes to combine the flavors; then taste and adjust the seasonings. Sprinkle with chopped cilantro and serve with basmati rice alongside.

★ ★
NOTE

Instead of—or in addition to—rice, serve this Anglo-Indian dish with *paratha* or naan bread, both of which you can buy at specialty or gourmet markets.

ASIAN GAZPACHO

MAKES 1 QUART, SERVES 6

Today, a few miles from my mom's house in Los Altos, California, generations-old peach orchards have now been supplanted by high-tech Apple computers. Yet it's apropos that one of the most popular products to have come out of Silicon Valley is named after a fruit; after all, this region's bounty has always been local and sustainable. At the same time, the South Bay is home to a large Asian population—many of the area's remaining farmers are third- or fourth-generation Asians—and so Asian greens are readily abundant at the local farmer's market, where Early Girl tomatoes sit side by side with lemongrass and Thai holy basil. When putting together a late-summer gazpacho, I grabbed a handful of the best-looking seasonal produce and herbs I could find there. The result was this umami-packed gazpacho—a riff on the classic Spanish cold soup.

In a food processor or blender, puree the tomatoes with the cucumbers, red onion, garlic, and ginger for 30 seconds or until smooth. Pour the gazpacho into a large bowl. Add the sesame oil, mirin, and sea salt to taste. If using Sriracha, add a few drops to taste.

Serve immediately, or even better, refrigerate for several hours to let the flavors blend. Just before serving, stir in the Thai basil, cilantro, scallions, and a squeeze of lime. Garnish each serving with sesame seeds.

4 ripe medium **tomatoes** (about 1½ pounds)

2 **cucumbers**, peeled and chopped

1 small **red onion**, chopped (⅓ cup)

2 **garlic cloves**, minced

1 1-inch knob fresh **ginger**, minced

¼ cup **Asian sesame oil**

¼ cup **mirin**

Sea salt, to taste

Sriracha or other tangy chili sauce, to taste (optional)

½ cup fresh **Thai basil leaves**

½ cup fresh **cilantro leaves**, chopped

2 **scallions** (green and white parts), thinly sliced

Lime wedges

Toasted sesame seeds, for garnish

RICE BOWLS AND BEYOND

GRANDMA HSIANG'S
CHINESE TAMALES
Page 149

When I decided to create a pan-Asian food festival, I named it LUCKYRICE because both luck and rice are universal signifiers across Asian cultures; from India to Korea, China to Singapore, we feast on rice and revere the concept of luck. Rice feeds us, literally and symbolically, keeping us nourished and spirited. In reverence, we offer rice to the Chinese kitchen god to ward away evil spirits, and to the Chinese god of farming, for a prosperous harvest. We usher in newlyweds by throwing rice at them so that they may never go hungry, and in Japan, rice wine is sipped at the end of the wedding ceremony to seal the union.

Pounded sticky rice or *mochi* is almost always served in some form at New Year celebrations; it's a metaphorical glue, if you will, that represents the wish for keeping friends and families together in the future. In Singapore, an iron rice bowl symbolizes a job well done, whereas a broken rice bowl is a sign of being out of work. This almighty grain is valuable even in the afterlife: We offer rice to our ancestors by placing bowls of it on their shrines, to ensure that they are well fed.

If there's one food I can't live without, it's rice. Neither, however, can most of our Earth's hungriest, many of whom subsist largely on rice. Indeed, rice is a poor person's food, and as countries like China and India continue to become richer and more urbanized, rice consumption there has actually decreased because more people can afford a diversified diet. Still, with 90 percent of all rice consumed and produced in Asia, rice farming is critical to Asian agriculture and tradition. The Japanese emperor, for instance, continues to grow a symbolic plot of rice and leads the nation in its annual harvesting festivities.

When it comes to food, rice, of course, is the foundation of Asian cuisine, whether Korean bibimbap (see opposite), Japanese sushi (see page 153), or Chinese congee (see page 155). Such dishes also showcase the spectrum of rice varietals, from Thai jasmine and Japanese short-grain to Indian basmati. Rice is the Asian staff of life—so much so that instead of asking "How are you?" many Asian cultures greet one another with "Have you eaten your rice yet?"

BIBIMBAP

SERVES 4

The Koreans have a tradition of stirring together all the food offerings made at an ancestral rite and then eating the mixture. This is likely the basis of bibimbap (or "mixed rice"), where an artful composition of meats and vegetables on steamed rice is blended with a *gochujang* sauce. This kaleidoscope of ingredients is also rich in symbolism: black seaweed and shiitake mushrooms represent the north and the kidneys; reddish ingredients including carrots stand for the south and the heart; green cucumbers and spinach call out to the east and the liver; and white rice and bean sprouts evoke the west and the lungs. Lastly, the yellow egg yolks represent the center and the stomach.

MAKE THE SAUCE: Mix the *gochujang,* sesame oil, brown sugar, vinegar, garlic, and 1 tablespoon of water together in a small bowl. Set aside.

MARINATE THE MEAT: In a medium bowl, mix together the garlic, soy sauce, sesame oil, and brown sugar. Add the beef strips and let the beef marinate for 10 to 15 minutes.

PREPARE THE RICE: Heat the vegetable oil in a cast-iron skillet over medium heat, swirling to coat the bottom of the skillet. Add the rice and pat it into an even layer. Reduce the heat to medium-low and let the rice cook, without stirring, for 10 to 15 minutes, until it has a crispy golden crust on the bottom.

PREPARE THE TOPPINGS: While the rice is cooking, heat 1 tablespoon of the vegetable oil in a wok or skillet over medium heat, and add the spinach. Sprinkle it lightly with sea salt and cook, stirring frequently, for 3 to 4 minutes, until softened and tender. Transfer the spinach to a bowl and set aside.

recipe continues

FOR THE SAUCE:

¼ cup **gochujang** chili paste

1 tablespoon **Asian sesame oil**

1 tablespoon **light brown sugar**

1 teaspoon **rice vinegar**

1 small **garlic clove**, minced

FOR THE MEAT:

2 **garlic cloves**, minced

1 tablespoon **soy sauce**

1 tablespoon **Asian sesame oil**

1 teaspoon **light brown sugar**

6 ounces **beef round steak**,
     cut into thin strips

FOR THE RICE:

1 tablespoon **vegetable oil**

6 cups **cooked rice**

Add ½ tablespoon of the vegetable oil to the same pan, and cook the shiitake mushrooms over medium heat for 2 to 3 minutes, until they have softened and the edges are lightly browned. Add the soy sauce and cook until any visible liquid has evaporated and the mushrooms are lightly glazed. Set them aside in a small bowl.

Add another ½ tablespoon vegetable oil to the pan, add the bean sprouts, and sprinkle them lightly with sea salt. Cook for 1 minute, to just heat through and soften slightly. Set aside.

Heat a little more vegetable oil in the same pan, and fry the 4 eggs, sunny side up or over easy as desired. Divide the rice among 4 large bowls and set the fried eggs on top of the rice.

Remove the beef from the marinade. Working quickly, add a bit more oil to the pan and cook the beef over high heat, tossing it until it is cooked through and lightly browned, 3 to 4 minutes. Divide the beef among the serving bowls, placing it next to the egg, and then arrange the spinach, cucumber, mushrooms, seaweed, sprouts, and shredded carrots, in separate heaps, around the beef and egg.

Serve with the *gochujang* sauce on the side, so diners can stir the ingredients together with as much sauce as desired.

FOR THE TOPPINGS:

2 to 3 tablespoons **vegetable oil**

1 10-ounce bag fresh **spinach leaves**, washed, large stems discarded

Sea salt, to taste

6 fresh **shiitake mushrooms**, thinly sliced

½ cup **nori seaweed**, cut into about 1-inch-wide strips

1 tablespoon **soy sauce**

1½ cups **mung bean sprouts**

4 large **eggs**

1 medium **Persian cucumber**, unpeeled and cut in half lengthwise, then into thin strips

1 large **carrot**, shredded

PERFECT STEAMED RICE

MAKES 4 CUPS, SERVES 6

A recipe for steamed rice seems unnecessary: add rice and water to rice cooker, turn on. But while that is a reliable way to make consistently good rice, I also like to cook rice the way our ancestors did. Making perfect steamed rice is a badge of honor that many chefs toil at for years—no, decades—before humbly mastering. There are, of course, hundreds of varieties of rice, each of which will call for its own cooking method. Here is a traditional recipe for steaming short-grain rice with a creamy, almost sticky texture. To add flair to dinner parties, try serving rice in a bamboo steamer lined with napa cabbage leaves to keep the grains from falling through.

14 ounces (1¾ cups) uncooked **short-grain rice**

Place the rice in a heavy pot and add water to cover by about 1 inch. Cover the pot with a tight-fitting lid and steam the rice, without stirring, at a steady boil, until most of the water has been absorbed, about 25 minutes.

Keeping the cover on, reduce the heat to low and let the rice sit undisturbed for another 5 minutes. Serve hot.

★ ★ TIP Rinsing rice before cooking removes surface starch, which prevents stickiness, but doing so will wash away vitamins and nutrients. With short-grain rice, where a bit of toothy starchiness is a good thing, there is no need to pre-rinse.

GRILLED STICKY RICE-ON-A-STICK

Dango

SERVES 6

Sticky rice treats are a staple in many Asian cuisines—as a sweet snack, as dessert, or in lieu of a bowl of rice as part of a meal. As a snack, Japanese sweets (*wagashi*) such as these *dango* are served particularly at celebrations like Children's Day on May 5. These grilled rice balls are made with a mixture of sweet glutinous rice flour and plain rice flour. Using a combination helps in shaping the *dango* (they'd be soft and gooey if made with just the sweet rice flour).

In a bowl, combine the two rice flours with the 2 teaspoons of sugar. Gradually stir 1 cup of warm water into the mixture, and knead slowly in the bowl until the dough becomes smooth. Divide the dough into 24 balls, about ¾ inch in diameter. Bring a large pot of water to a boil, and set up an ice bath. Boil the *dango* for about 2 minutes, until the balls float to the surface. Remove the *dango* and plunge them into the ice bath. Drain well.

Soak 6 bamboo skewers in water for about 10 minutes. Thread 4 rice balls onto each skewer. Oil a cast-iron skillet or grill pan with the vegetable oil, and heat it over medium-high heat. Place the skewers on the skillet and cook, slowly rotating them to char the rice balls, about 4 minutes.

Combine the 5 tablespoons of sugar, the soy sauce, mirin, and ¼ cup of water in a small saucepan and bring to a boil, stirring occasionally, over medium-high heat. Add the cornstarch, and stir until the sauce thickens, about 3 minutes. Remove from the heat. Place the skewers on a serving platter. Brush some of the soy sauce glaze over the rice balls to coat them, and then repeat with a second coating. Serve immediately.

½ cup **rice flour**

½ cup **sweet glutinous rice flour**

2 teaspoons **sugar** for the dough, plus 5 tablespoons sugar for the glaze

2 tablespoons **vegetable oil**, for grilling

1 tablespoon **soy sauce**

1 tablespoon **mirin**

1 tablespoon **cornstarch**

CLAY POT MUSHROOM RISOTTO

SERVES 6

Clay pots are ideal for slow-cooked dishes across the Asian spectrum, from Japanese *donabe* to Vietnamese *kho*, but this recipe was inspired by the Italian method of cooking risotto, where broth is added a ladle at a time so that the rice fully absorbs the liquid. It made me wonder, what if this classic technique was used in an Asian clay pot, which is unglazed on the outside but glazed on the inside so that little moisture is lost during the cooking process? This is the delicious answer to that question, a marriage of Italian techniques and Asian cookery. My motto for this dish is always "the more the merrier" when it comes to the mushrooms (in terms of both quantity and variety), as they add a meaty, earthy goodness to the dish. And don't skimp on the soy sauce and scallions—they really tie the flavors together.

Heat the olive oil in a clay pot over medium heat. Add the garlic and stir until fragrant, about 30 seconds. Add the mushrooms and cook, stirring, until they have softened and released their juices, about 3 minutes. Add the brown rice and cook, stirring it in the juices from the mushrooms, until the grains have visibly absorbed some of the cooking liquid, about 3 minutes. Add the chicken broth, one cup at a time, so that the rice absorbs the cooking liquid (similar to how you would make risotto), and simmer until the rice is al dente, about 35 minutes.

Arrange the sausage slices uniformly on top of the rice, cover the clay pot, and let it steam for 5 to 10 minutes, until the sausage is heated through. The rice should be slightly crispy and browned on the bottom, and it will be scented with the smoky flavor of the sausage. Stir it well just before serving, making sure to scrape up the rice crust on the bottom of the clay pot. Serve the "risotto" in individual bowls, and let your guests scatter scallions and sprinkle soy sauce on top as they desire.

2 tablespoons **olive oil**

2 **garlic cloves**, minced

3 cups coarsely chopped **assorted fresh mushrooms** (such as cremini, shiitakes, oysters, portobellos)

1½ cups uncooked **short-grain brown rice**

4 cups **chicken broth**

6 links **Chinese smoked sausage** (*lap cheong*), cut into ¼-inch-thick slices (see Tip)

Thinly sliced **scallions** (green and white parts), for garnish

Soy sauce, for serving

★ ★ TIP

The quality of the sausage you buy makes a huge difference here. Good Chinese *lap cheong* sausages have a meaty smokiness that's reminiscent of Virginia country ham.

GRANDMA HSIANG'S CHINESE TAMALES

Zongzi
MAKES 12 ZONGZI

Zongzi, often referred to as "Chinese tamales," are traditional sticky rice bundles stuffed with treasures like cured pork belly, juicy Chinese sausage, salted duck egg yolks, or dried baby shrimp and scallops—all beautifully wrapped in aromatic bamboo leaves like a present. This is my maternal grandmother's perfect streamlined version of the treat sold by Shanghainese street food vendors. She likes to feed us *zongzi*, saying, "You young people are so skinny and too busy to eat."

I now realize that she learned how to make *zongzi* only after she moved to America and grew homesick for the beloved comfort foods of her childhood. There's nothing that causes homesickness—or perhaps soothes it—more than the smells of food from home. So to feed her nostalgia, she learned how to cook *zongzi* for herself, and to this day, at 99 years of age, my grandmother still makes these edible gifts for my mom and her five siblings, along with her myriad lucky grandchildren and great-grandchildren.

MAKE THE FILLING: In a large bowl, combine the soy sauce, rice wine, cinnamon stick, star anise, and five-spice powder. Add the pork belly and stir well. Then cover the bowl with plastic wrap and marinate in the refrigerator for at least 2 hours or as long as overnight.

PREPARE THE RICE: Put the glutinous rice in a large bowl and add cold water to cover. Let it stand at room temperature, covered, for as long as 2 hours.

recipe continues

FOR THE FILLING:

5 tablespoons **soy sauce**

2 tablespoons **Shaoxing rice wine**

1 1-inch piece **cinnamon stick**

2 **star anise pods**

1 teaspoon **five-spice powder**, homemade (see page 60) or store-bought

2 pounds **pork belly**, cut into 1-inch cubes

FOR THE *ZONGZI*:

3 cups uncooked **sweet glutinous rice**

24 **dried bamboo leaves**

3 tablespoons **soy sauce**

2 tablespoons **vegetable oil**

6 **shallots**, sliced

12 fresh **shiitake mushrooms**, thinly sliced

Rinse the bamboo leaves and soak them in a bowl of hot water for 30 minutes. Drain and set aside.

Drain the rice and return the grains to the bowl. Add the soy sauce and stir to combine. Set aside.

Heat the vegetable oil in a medium skillet over medium heat, add the shallots and mushrooms, and fry for 3 to 4 minutes, until softened and lightly colored.

ASSEMBLE THE *ZONGZI:* Place 2 bamboo leaves, overlapping, on a clean surface to make a 5-inch-wide piece. Fold 2 to 3 inches of the stem inward to form a straight edge. Cup the rectangular end in your hand, and place 1 tablespoon of the rice in the "cup." Spread the rice out about 3 inches toward the leaf tip.

Remove the meat from the marinade. Place 2 pieces of meat directly on top of the rice, and add 1 tablespoon of the shallot-mushroom mixture. Spread 2 tablespoons of the rice over the meat so it is completely enveloped by the rice. Bring the other side of the leaf over the rice-filled cup to enclose it. Wrap a 2-foot-long piece of kitchen twine several times around the middle of each *zongzi,* tying it off with a knot, so the rice won't escape during the cooking process. Repeat with the remaining bamboo leaves, rice, and filling.

Place all the *zongzi* in a large pot, and add water to cover by 1 inch. Cover the pot and bring to a boil; then reduce the heat to low and cook the *zongzi* for 3 hours. (Make sure there is enough water to cover the *zongzi* at all times, adding more as necessary.) Transfer the cooked *zongzi* to a plate and let them cool slightly.

When you are ready to eat, cut off the string, unfold, and dig in!

The cooked *zongzi* can be kept in the refrigerator for a week, or frozen for months. Simply thaw the *zongzi* if they are frozen, and steam them for about 10 minutes or until heated through.

PLAY WITH YOUR FOOD

There's a Japanese food import that's the current talk of the town, and it's not ramen—it's bento boxes. Instead of hipster foodies, this time the obsession has found resonance with the "mommy" set, who have taken to making cute bento boxes for their kids and then blogging to their legions of fans. The Consulate General of Japan in Los Angeles along with Bento USA launched a popular "Cute Character Bento Photo Contest" as a way to celebrate Japan's cute and cool food culture, a source of national pride that even made UNESCO's 2013 Intangible Cultural Heritage of Humanity List.

Of course there's nothing new about bento boxes, which are as commonplace in Japan, Taiwan, and elsewhere in Asia as the brown-bagged lunch is in the United States. It's what housewives send their kids and spouses off with every day, or pick up for themselves from bento lunch stands. Standard bento boxes usually contain rice (maybe an *onigiri*, a rice ball sometimes stuffed with some salmon or *ume* plum paste and wrapped in seaweed), a piece of broiled fish, and some pickles. From there, things can get more elaborate. *Bento* originates from the Chinese word *biandong*, meaning "ordinary," but the new craze surrounding meticulously made character bentos (*kyara-ben*) or picture bentos (*oekakiben*) is anything but. A whole cottage industry has sprung up selling molds and tools to help shape rice, eggs, vegetables, and meats into cute characters.

Back in Japan, the current bento box craze is less surprising given how cuteness (*kawaii*) is a powerful element of Japanese pop culture—where men carry Miffy cell phone cases and icons like Hello Kitty (which today is an $8 billion business!) target grown-ups, not their kids. After all, Japan is where the cool culture of anime and manga was also born. Ladies and gentlemen, it's okay to play with your food again.

DIY SUSHI HAND ROLLS

Temaki

MAKES 24 TEMAKI ROLLS, SERVES 4 TO 6

For the Japanese, sushi is a venerable art form, something best left in the hands of sushi masters instead of home cooks. On the other hand, *temaki* sushi (or hand rolls) are an easy way to bring this tradition home. To prepare this sushi feast, arrange rice, nori, a variety of sashimi-grade fish (tuna, salmon, yellowtail, and salmon roe are my go-to, but get whatever is the freshest), and vegetable fillings on a platter so that everyone can make their own hand rolls. Provide small bowls of soy sauce and wasabi for dipping. I like to serve this feast when I'm entertaining at home; rolling these cones of sushi is as fun for little hands as it is delicious for grown-up guests.

12 sheets **nori seaweed**, cut in half

6 cups cooked **Japanese sushi rice** (see Note)

3 pounds **sashimi-grade fish** (see headnote), sliced into narrow 2-inch-long strips

6 cups **assorted fillings**, such as cucumber and carrot strips, shiso leaves, radish sprouts, sliced avocado, and pickled daikon strips

Soy sauce

Grated fresh wasabi (see headnote, page 99) or wasabi paste from a tube (available at Asian groceries)

Pickled ginger

To assemble a hand roll, lay a piece of nori flat on a clean surface. Spread a thin layer of sushi rice on the left side of the nori. Add the fish and vegetable fillings vertically down the middle of the rice (it's okay if they poke out of the seaweed). Fold the bottom left corner of the nori upward to create a cone shape, and then roll from one side of the nori to the other until all of the seaweed is shaped into a cone. Moisten the outer edge of the roll with a bit of water or a morsel of rice, and press to seal.

Serve soy sauce, wasabi, and pickled ginger alongside.

★ ★ NOTE   Sushi rice is high-quality Japanese short-grain rice (which is slightly sticky when cooked); long-grain rice will not do.

SAVORY RICE BALLS

Nuo Mi Fan

SERVES 8 AS AN HORS D'OEUVRE

Sticky rice studded with Chinese sausages and black mushrooms makes a great stuffing for roasted duck or a Thanksgiving turkey. But this stuffing can also be sculpted into mini rice balls (almost like dim sum) for passed hors d'oeuvres at cocktail gatherings.

2 cups uncooked **sticky rice**

2 tablespoons **soy sauce**

2 tablespoons **Asian sesame oil**

6 large **dried black mushrooms**

2 tablespoons **vegetable oil**

1 teaspoon **sugar**

5 tablespoons minced **shallots**

4 links **Chinese smoked sausage** (*lap cheong*), cut into small dice

Fresh **cilantro leaves**, for garnish (optional)

Rinse the rice thoroughly in a sieve, drain it well, and then place it in a medium bowl. Add cold water to cover and let the rice soak for at least 2 hours or as long as overnight.

Drain the rice thoroughly and place it in a rice cooker on the sticky rice setting. Stir in the soy sauce and sesame oil, and steam until tender, about 25 minutes.

Meanwhile, place the dried mushrooms in a medium bowl and add hot water to cover. Let them soak for about 30 minutes, until softened. Then drain and slice them into thin strips.

Heat the vegetable oil in a wok over medium-high heat. Add the sugar, shallots, mushrooms, and sausages and stir-fry until fragrant, 2 to 3 minutes.

Stir the cooked rice into the sausage mixture. Remove from the heat and let the mixture cool to room temperature, or until it is not too hot to touch.

Mold the rice mixture into 1-inch balls, wetting your hands with cold water after forming each ball to prevent stickiness. Spread the finished balls on a baking sheet and cover with plastic wrap for up to 30 minutes until ready to serve. If desired, garnish with cilantro just before serving.

TURKEY CONGEE

SERVES 6 TO 8

My all-time favorite breakfast is a nourishing bowl of congee (or *jook* in Cantonese), which is as common in parts of China and Japan as cereal is in the United States. Congee is usually made with plain water and rice, but it is much better when prepared with a savory broth—the kind that has been slow-simmered with lots of bones, like those of a turkey carcass. In fact, I insist on roasting a turkey at Thanksgiving every year because the leftover meat and bones make a gobble-worthy congee for the entire holiday weekend. If you have some leftover cooked vegetables (black or shiitake mushrooms are great), add them when you stir in the turkey meat at the end.

1 small leftover **turkey carcass** (2 to 3 pounds)

4 **scallions**, green and white parts chopped, plus more for garnish

1 2-inch knob fresh **ginger**, slightly bruised

1 cup uncooked **jasmine rice**

Soy sauce (optional)

Ground white pepper (optional)

Coarsely chopped fresh **cilantro leaves**, for garnish

Place the turkey carcass in a stockpot and add about 3 quarts of water to cover. Add the scallions and the ginger, and set the pot over medium heat. Cover and let simmer for about 2 hours.

Strain the broth through a colander into a large pot; discard the bones and set aside any meat. (You will have about 3 quarts of broth.) Stir the rice into the broth and let it simmer, covered, until the rice is broken down to a creamy porridge, about 1 hour.

To serve, stir in the reserved meat. Season with soy sauce and white pepper, if needed, and garnish with scallions and cilantro.

★ ★
TIP

The key to delicious fried rice
is to use leftover rice that's been
refrigerated overnight, so that it
is dried out and less sticky.

INDONESIAN FRIED RICE

Nasi Goreng

SERVES 4

Fried rice is always a crowd-pleaser, and you'll find this famous dish everywhere in Indonesia: on tin plates at roadside stands and on fine porcelain at Jakarta dinner parties. Spiced with sweet soy sauce, shallots, garlic, shrimp paste, and chiles, and tossed with egg and chicken, this aromatic one-dish meal is actually a breakfast favorite. For added crunch, serve it with fried shallots and prawn crackers.

½ cup **vegetable oil**

1 large boneless, skinless **chicken breast**, cut into 4 pieces

4 **shallots**, halved

4 **garlic cloves**

1 **lemongrass stalk**, trimmed, bruised, and coarsely chopped

1 teaspoon *belacan shrimp paste*

4 fresh **Thai red chiles**, seeds removed

2 large **eggs**, beaten

5 cups day-old cooked **long-grain rice** (see headnote)

¼ cup *kecap manis* (Indonesian sweet soy sauce)

1 tablespoon **soy sauce**

4 fried **eggs**

3 **scallions** (green and white parts), thinly sliced

Fried shallots (optional)

Prawn crackers (optional)

Line a bowl with paper towels and set it aside. Heat the vegetable oil in a wok over high heat until it is nearly smoking. Carefully add the chicken pieces and cook for 5 to 6 minutes, turning them occasionally, until they are well fried and dark brown on all sides. Transfer the chicken to the paper towel–lined bowl and let it cool. When it is cool enough to handle, shred the meat into small pieces and set aside. Remove all but 2 tablespoons of the oil from the wok.

In a food processor, process the shallots, garlic, lemongrass, *belacan,* and Thai chiles to form a smooth paste. (If the mixture is too dry to process, add 1 to 2 tablespoons water, being careful not to over-wet it.)

Heat the reserved oil in the wok over medium heat. Add the shallot paste and fry it for 2 to 3 minutes, until fragrant and darkened in color. Push the fried paste to one side of the pan, pour in the beaten eggs, and cook for 1 to 2 minutes to firm up. Break up the cooked egg and mix it with the fried paste. Add the rice and the shredded chicken to the wok and stir-fry for 3 to 4 minutes, mixing them with the egg. Stir in the *kecap manis* and soy sauce, and cook, stirring constantly, for 3 minutes, until the ingredients are combined. Divide the rice among 4 bowls and top each serving with a fried egg, scallions, and fried shallots and prawn crackers, if using.

★ ★ NOTE

Fried shallots and prawn crackers can be found at Asian grocery stores.

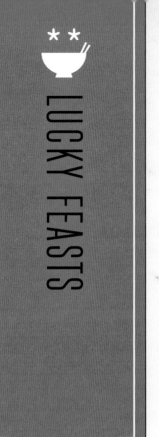

LUCKY FEASTS

WHOLE STEAMED FISH
Page 177

Given the long list of lucky foods in Chinese culture, one might suppose that the path to good fortune starts with the stomach: noodles for longevity, eggs for fertility, whole fish for abundance, candy for sweetness, tangerines for luck, and oranges for wealth. A large part of my identity has to do with the things I ate at the family dinner table, and since I grew up learning about my Chinese heritage through food, this chapter focuses on lucky feasts primarily through the lens of Chinese culture.

However, as I've chowed down with friends, family, and sometimes strangers, I have learned that every culture has its own set of lucky foods to celebrate the New Year: Italians eat round lentils (which look like ancient Roman coins) to usher in good fortune and Jewish families serve foods with apples and honey—sweet treats for a sweet start to the year. How interesting that feasting imbues often-humble foods with auspiciousness!

Around Chinese festivities, a key component to these celebrations is about communal eating; banquet tables are designed for jolly groups of ten to share lucky dishes (usually served as eight courses since eight is a lucky number). Gathering with friends and family is central to these festivities, especially during New Year's Day, an occasion which is celebrated around the world with lucky foods in late January or early February (according to the lunar calendar, which changes every year).

In Chinese homes, a traditional must-eat food on New Year's Eve is dumplings (or *jiaozi* in Mandarin), which families wrap together and eat as the clock strikes midnight. Dumplings symbolize longevity and wealth; their shape resembles gold shoe-shaped ingots, an early form of Chinese currency. Sometimes we'll actually stuff coins into random dumplings so that a chance encounter while eating one of these dumplings brings the promise of prosperity. Even more than eating the dumplings themselves, I look forward to the wrapping party, where everyone joins in to manifest good fortune for the year to come.

I may or may not be able to influence luck, but I'll take my chances with our dumpling ritual every year. If luck has it, this Chinese family tradition—and my cultural heritage—will endure, and *that* is a feast worth celebrating.

CLASSIC CHINESE DUMPLINGS

Jiaozi

MAKES ABOUT 24 DUMPLINGS

From Polish *pierogi* to Italian *ravioli* to pan-fried Japanese *gyoza*, dumplings are universal comfort food. Even though there are as many variations as there are eaters, the classic Chinese dumpling is filled with a pork and garlic chive base to which cabbage, scallions, and other ingredients such as black mushrooms can be added. Chinese dumplings can also be cooked in a multitude of ways—most traditionally boiled (*shuijiao*, which literally means "water dumpling"), but also steamed (*zhengjiao*) and pan-fried (*guotie*, commonly known as "pot stickers").

MAKE THE DUMPLING FILLING: Coarsely chop the cabbage, and then transfer it to a food processor. Pulse until the cabbage is finely chopped but not pureed. Remove the cabbage, wrap it in a clean kitchen towel, and squeeze it to remove any excess liquid. Transfer the cabbage to a large bowl and stir in the pork, scallions, garlic chives, garlic, ginger, soy sauce, and sesame oil. If you wish to taste for seasoning, poach or fry a small amount of the filling, and adjust the seasonings to your liking.

SHAPE THE DUMPLINGS: Holding a dumpling wrapper flat in your hand, place 2 teaspoons of the filling in the center of the wrapper. Wet the edges of the wrapper and fold the dumpling in half to form a half-moon shape, pressing out the air as you seal the dumpling. Use your fingers to pinch pleats around the edge of the half circle. Repeat until all the filling is used.

recipe continues

FOR THE DUMPLING FILLING:

½ pound **napa cabbage** (about ¼ head), plus extra leaves for lining the steamer

½ pound **ground pork**

½ bunch **scallions** (green and white parts), finely chopped

½ cup chopped **garlic chives**

1 large **garlic clove**, finely chopped

1 1-inch knob fresh **ginger**, grated

3 tablespoons **soy sauce**

½ teaspoon **Asian sesame oil**

½ pound round **wheat dumpling wrappers**

FOR THE DIPPING SAUCE:

¼ cup **soy sauce**

2 tablespoons **rice vinegar**

1 teaspoon thinly sliced **scallions**, white part only

¼ teaspoon **toasted sesame seeds**

½ teaspoon freshly **ground black pepper**

COOK THE DUMPLINGS: Here are three different ways to prepare dumplings.

Boil: Boiling dumplings is the most traditional way to cook them. To do so, bring a large pot of water to a slow boil. Add the dumplings and cook until they float to the surface. Then add about a cup of cold water. When the water returns to a boil, add another cup of cold water. When the dumplings float to the surface again, use a slotted spoon to remove them to a platter.

Steam: Pour about 2 inches of water into a wide pot or a wok, and bring to a boil. Arrange the dumplings in a single layer in a bamboo steamer lined with the extra napa cabbage leaves or parchment paper. Cover the steamer, place it in the pot (don't let the water touch the dumplings), and cook at a low heat for about 5 minutes, until cooked through.

Pan-fry: Heat a nonstick pan over high heat. Add 2 tablespoons vegetable oil and swirl it around; then add the dumplings in one layer without letting them touch. Add enough water to reach halfway up the dumplings. Cover the pan and cook over medium-high heat until all the water has evaporated and the bottoms are browned and crispy.

MAKE THE DIPPING SAUCE: While the dumplings are boiling, steaming, or frying, combine the soy sauce with the rice vinegar, scallions, sesame seeds, and black pepper in a small bowl. Serve the dumplings hot, with the sauce on the side.

TIP
If you are not cooking them immediately, freeze the dumplings for up to 3 months. To do so, place dumplings on a baking sheet lined with parchment paper and freeze them for about an hour before transferring them to a sealed freezer bag.

STEAMED TURNIP CAKES

Law Bok Gow

SERVES 6 AS PART OF A LARGER DIM SUM MEAL

A staple of dim sum carts, turnip cakes are an auspicious New Year food because the Chinese word for daikon radish is a homophone for "good fortune." Even though the name of this dish references turnips, it is actually made with Chinese daikon radish, whose flavor resembles that of a turnip. The most popular, and more traditional, way to eat these slightly sweet turnip cakes is to pan-fry the steamed slices until golden brown. An alternative cooking method to frying is to make a softer, more liquid version that is eaten steamed with a spoon by adding more daikon and less rice flour. To turn this rather humble dish into something extravagant, top the steamed turnip cake with the luscious dried scallops found in Asian grocery stores.

---

8 **dried shiitake mushrooms**

½ cup **dried shrimp**

1 large **daikon** (about 2 pounds)

2 tablespoons **vegetable oil**, plus more for frying

6 ounces **Chinese smoked sausage** (*lap cheong*), diced

2 tablespoons **Shaoxing rice wine**

1 tablespoon **sugar**

2 cups **rice flour**

½ teaspoon **sea salt**

6 medium **dried scallops**, rehydrated and shredded by hand (optional)

Place the dried mushrooms and shrimp in separate bowls. Pour ½ cup of hot water over the mushrooms, and pour ½ cup of cold water over the shrimp. Set the bowls aside for 30 minutes.

Grate the daikon into a large pot. Add 4 cups of water and bring to a boil. Reduce the heat to a simmer and cook for 30 minutes, until the daikon is tender. Drain the daikon in a colander set over a large bowl, reserving the cooking liquid. Transfer the drained daikon to a large pot.

Set the colander over a clean bowl, and drain the shrimp and mushrooms in the colander, catching the soaking liquids below. Squeeze any excess liquid out of the mushrooms into the bowl; reserve the liquid. Finely chop the mushrooms and the shrimp.

In a wok or a large pan, heat the 2 tablespoons vegetable oil over medium heat. Add the sausage and fry until cooked through and lightly browned, about 10 minutes. Add the mushrooms and shrimp, and stir-fry for 2 minutes. Add the rice wine and sugar, and stir to dissolve the sugar. Remove the wok from the heat and stir the mixture into the cooked daikon.

In a large bowl, combine the rice flour with the reserved mushroom/shrimp soaking liquid, and stir until smooth. Add the sea salt and 1 cup of the reserved daikon broth. Then add the daikon-sausage mixture and mix until well combined.

Spread the mixture out in a shallow 8-inch round heatproof or Pyrex bowl. Bring about 2 inches of water to a boil in a wide pan or a wok. Place the bowl in a bamboo steamer, set the steamer in the pan (do not let the water touch the bowl), cover the steamer, and steam at medium heat for 1 hour or until the turnip cake is firm to the touch. (If using dried scallops, add them to the top of the cake during the last 10 minutes of steaming.)

Remove the bowl from the steamer and allow the turnip cake to cool at room temperature. When it has cooled, run a knife along the edge of the cake to loosen it, and turn it out right-side up onto a plate. If not eating immediately, wrap the turnip cake in plastic wrap and refrigerate for up to one week. When ready to eat, coat a frying pan with oil on medium heat. Meanwhile, cut the cake into 1-inch-thick slices and about the length of a playing card, and add to the pan. Fry on each side for about 5 minutes, or until the turnip cakes develop a golden brown hue. Serve warm.

NOTE

You'll find this dish along with steamed dumplings and delicacies like chicken feet in black bean sauce on carts at dim sum restaurants. Dim sum is a Chinese brunch tradition that literally means "to touch your heart." To me, dim sum means "then some"—it's leisure time to gossip with friends while nibbling. The food is *almost* secondary to the gathering; the cacophonous atmosphere of a large dim sum hall, the high-octane rattle of carts making their cheerful rounds, and of course, the sound of loud laughter and happy eating taking over each table, this is where the real action is.

CHRYSANTHEMUM AND TOFU SALAD

Ma Lan Tou
SERVES 6

Not to be confused with the Sichuanese dish *ma po tofu, ma lan tou* is a refreshing and easy-to-compose cold salad that is frequently served as part of a selection of small plates at the start of a Shanghainese feast. Along with crumbled firm tofu, chrysanthemum leaves (known as *shungiku* leaves in Japanese, or *tong ho* in Cantonese) are the co-star of the dish. They impart a fragrant and mildly grassy note to this herbaceous salad, and are easily found in Asian groceries (particularly when in season, from spring to autumn). Excellent raw, young chrysanthemum greens are also a great addition to soups and the Japanese hot pot, *shabu shabu.*

Whisk the soy sauce, vinegar, sugar, sea salt, white pepper, and sesame oil together in a small bowl.

Combine the chrysanthemum leaves, cilantro, and scallions in a large bowl.

In another large bowl, crumble the tofu with your hands. Add the salad mixture to the tofu and toss to combine. Then add the dressing, toss, and let the salad marinate for about 15 minutes in the refrigerator to let the flavors mingle. Do not leave the dressed salad for more than an hour, or the greens will start to wilt. Serve the salad chilled.

¼ cup **light soy sauce**

1 tablespoon **rice vinegar**

1 tablespoon **sugar**

1 teaspoon **sea salt**

1 teaspoon **ground white pepper**

¼ cup **Asian sesame oil**

1 bunch **chrysanthemum leaves**, thick stems discarded, leaves finely chopped (about 2 cups)

½ bunch fresh **cilantro**, stems discarded and leaves coarsely chopped (about 1 cup)

2 **scallions** (green and white parts), finely chopped

1 pound **firm tofu**

★ ★
NOTE

This dish is for cilantro lovers. If you don't fall into that category, feel free to substitute flat-leaf parsley for the cilantro.

SHANGHAINESE DRUNKEN CHICKEN

Zui Ji

SERVES 10 AS PART OF A BANQUET MEAL

At banquets, guests are often greeted with a platter of assorted cold appetizers as they sit down to dinner. These small dishes are meant to whet your appetite and may include delicacies such as jellyfish salad, sliced roast pork, sweet mayonnaise prawns, preserved eggs, and of course, drunken chicken. To "intoxicate" the chicken, it is marinated in rice wine for up to 5 days, so this is a great dish for making ahead.

1 3-pound **chicken**

1 ½-inch knob fresh **ginger**, smashed

Sea salt, to taste

1½ cups **Shaoxing rice wine**

Fresh **cilantro sprigs**, for garnish

★ ★
TIP

Place the whole chicken and the ginger in a large pot, and add water to cover. Bring the water to a simmer, and cook, covered, over low heat until the chicken is just cooked through, about 30 minutes. (Be careful not to overcook it, or the meat will be dry and tough.) Remove the pot from the heat. Transfer chicken to a cutting board and allow it to cool. Skim the fat and debris from the chicken broth. Set aside 1 cup of the broth, and reserve the rest for another use.

When the chicken has cooled to the touch, discard the head, neck, feet, and gizzards. Chop the chicken "Chinese-style" into bite-size pieces. Place the chicken pieces, skin on, in a large bowl and season them generously with sea salt.

Pour the Shaoxing rice wine and the cup of reserved chicken broth over the chicken, and stir to coat. Cover the bowl with plastic wrap and let the chicken marinate in the refrigerator for at least 1 day or up to 5 days.

When you are ready to serve it, remove the chicken pieces from the marinade and discard the marinade. Serve the cold chicken pieces on a platter, garnished with a few sprigs of cilantro.

This dish will produce about 2 quarts of liquid from the poached chicken—which you should wisely save as a foundation for soups such as the Hot and Sour Soup (page 82) or Long Life "Supreme" Broth (page 79).

GARLICKY STIR-FRIED PEA SPROUTS

Chow Dau Miu

SERVES 6

At a Chinese banquet table covered with rich meaty dishes, a big plate of greens fresh from the wok is a perfect counterbalance. And around the New Year, green vegetables are a must-have since green is the color of money. This versatile recipe works with most tender leafy greens—including baby bok choy and *choy sum* (flowering cabbage)—so pick whatever looks best at the market. The crisp-tender shoots that grow abundantly from the snow peas, however, are my personal favorite. Once it is swirled into the garlic-scented oil, the fermented bean curd paste adds a layer of pungency to an otherwise straightforward dish.

2 tablespoons **vegetable oil**

6 to 10 **garlic cloves**, smashed

2 tablespoons **fermented bean curd paste**

1 pound **pea sprouts** (leaves and the tender curly shoots), picked over, rinsed, and patted dry

---

Heat a wok over high heat, and swirl in the vegetable oil. Add the garlic and stir-fry for 30 seconds; then add the bean curd paste. Add the pea sprouts and stir-fry for 5 minutes, until tender but still crisp. Serve right away.

CHAIRMAN MAO'S RED-BRAISED PORK BELLY

Hong Shao Rou

SERVES 4

Red-colored meats are eaten for good luck because red is the color of fire, a symbol of good fortune and joy. "Red cooking" is a Chinese method of stewing or braising with both dark and light soy sauces and caramelized sugar; it imparts a red color to the prepared food. Despite its appearance, dark soy sauce is actually not as salty as the light variety, and it is often the soy sauce of choice for hearty dishes like stews that require added body and color. Perhaps the most famous revolutionary dish from the Hunan province, this red-braised pork is symbolically tied to Chairman Mao Tse-tung because it was his favorite dish; supposedly he ate it every day.

1 pound **pork belly**, skin on

2 tablespoons **peanut oil**

2 tablespoons **sugar**

2 tablespoons **Shaoxing rice wine**

1 1-inch knob fresh **ginger**, sliced

1 **star anise pod**

¼ cup **dark soy sauce**

2 tablespoons **light soy sauce**

2 bunches **scallions**, green and white parts thinly sliced separately

Perfect Steamed Rice (page 145), for serving

Bring a large pot of water to a boil. Drop in the pork belly and cook for about 3 minutes to remove any impurities. Remove it from the water and cut it into 1-inch chunks.

In a wok, heat the peanut oil and sugar over low heat until the sugar caramelizes, about 10 minutes. Raise the heat to medium and add the cut-up pork. Cook for about 5 minutes, occasionally turning the pork so it is browned and well coated in the caramel.

Reduce the heat to low and add the rice wine, ginger, star anise, both soy sauces, the scallion whites, and ½ cup of water. Bring to a boil; then cover, reduce the heat, and simmer for about 1 hour, until the meat is fork-tender.

Uncover the pot and continue to cook the pork over low heat until it is coated with the syrup, about 15 minutes. Transfer the meat and sauce to a platter, and garnish with the scallion greens. Serve with steamed rice.

LION'S HEAD MEATBALLS WITH NAPA CABBAGE

Shih Tzu Tou

SERVES 4

This is a Shanghainese dish, reminiscent of the deep flavor of the region's slow-cooked dishes. These meatballs are popular fare across China, both as a home-cooked everyday dish and as a banquet specialty. If the title doesn't give it away, the large meatballs are meant to represent a lion and the shredded greens its wild mane. The finished dish will be brothy and aromatic, so I like to serve it over steamed rice. My favorite part of the dish is the cabbage broth that results from slow braising.

MAKE THE MEATBALLS: Place the mushrooms in a medium bowl, add hot water to cover, and soak for 30 minutes. Drain the mushrooms, reserving the soaking liquid, and squeeze them dry with your hands. Pour the reserved soaking liquid through a coffee filter–lined sieve (or a colander lined with a paper towel) into a bowl; reserve 1 cup of the liquid. Thinly slice the mushrooms.

In a large bowl, combine the pork, scallions, water chestnuts, rice wine, soy sauce, sesame oil, sugar, ginger, and kosher salt. Add the cornstarch and the beaten egg, and stir to combine. Form the mixture into 4 large meatballs. Transfer the meatballs to a plate and refrigerate until ready to cook.

Heat a large wok over high heat. Add the vegetable oil and heat it until it sizzles. Add the meatballs to the wok and cook for about 2 minutes; then rotate them so that the meatballs are browned all around, about 8 minutes total. (Depending on the size of your wok, you may have to do this in batches.) Set the meatballs aside on a clean plate.

FOR THE MEATBALLS:

8 **dried shiitake mushrooms**

1 pound **ground pork**

5 or 6 **scallions** (white and pale green parts), finely chopped, plus more for garnish

1 8-ounce can **water chestnuts**, drained and finely chopped

1 tablespoon **Shaoxing rice wine**

3 tablespoons **soy sauce**

2 tablespoons **Asian sesame oil**

1 tablespoon **sugar**

2 tablespoons finely chopped fresh **ginger**

1 teaspoon **kosher salt**, plus more for sprinkling

2 tablespoons **cornstarch**

1 large **egg**, beaten

2 tablespoons **vegetable oil**

MAKE THE CABBAGE: In the same wok, heat the vegetable oil over medium heat. Reserving about 1 cup of the cabbage, add the remaining cabbage, a handful at a time, to the wok and stir until wilted, 10 minutes. Nestle the meatballs down deep in the wilted cabbage and cover them with the remaining cup of uncooked cabbage. Top with the mushrooms. Sprinkle lightly with kosher salt and the black pepper, and pour the chicken broth over everything.

Cover the wok tightly and cook the meatballs and cabbage on low heat for 90 minutes, until the cabbage is meltingly tender. Garnish with the cilantro and additional scallions. Serve with hot steamed rice.

FOR THE CABBAGE:

2 tablespoons **vegetable oil**

1 head (about 3 pounds) **napa cabbage**, halved and cut into bite-size pieces

½ teaspoon freshly **ground black pepper**

1 cup **Long Life "Supreme" Broth** (page 79)

Chopped fresh **cilantro leaves**, for garnish

Perfect Steamed Rice (page 145), for serving

EATING (AND DRINKING) YOUR WAY THROUGH A CHINESE BANQUET

Chinese banquets mark the rhythms of life—birth, marriage, death—but these days, as China continues to prosper, it seems as though life is one endless banquet. More than an extravagant dinner party, banquets are feasts where not only do the dishes hold symbolism (be it wealth, long life, or happiness) but also a certain customary etiquette is expected of both the host and the guests.

For instance, banquets are served as a procession of eight lucky dishes since the number eight, *ba*, is a homophone for *fa*, which means "prosperity." First comes the cold platter of lucky delights, followed by an herbaceous chicken soup and a variety of meat dishes usually including a whole duck or chicken, greens, and a whole fish before a filling, starchy rice dish signals the impending finale to the feast. Instead of acting as an accompaniment to the other dishes, rice is served at the end of the meal so that guests can get their fill of the more expensive dishes that the host has proffered.

But above all else, banquets are thrown for good cheer. Toasting is mandatory; in fact, the first order of business for a good host is to get his guests spirited with drink—which often means shots of *baijiu*, known as "firewater," the world's most highly consumed spirit. The second: to honor his guests with a parade of food. I've met hosts who will save up for a year, subsisting on rice themselves, in order to afford luxury items—like rare herbs or expensive meat or fish—with which to regale their guests at a feast. In exchange, merry behavior is expected of good guests: to eat and drink in equal measure.

In Chinese culture, proper hosts always offer their guests more than they can eat, so don't be afraid to take home the leftovers; showing your appreciation is, after all, a sign of a good guest, no matter where you are.

LONGEVITY NOODLES

Yi Mein

SERVES 6

Noodles are a symbol of longevity and a must-have on birthdays throughout China—they carry the same symbolism as a birthday cake. Just as it's bad luck to share your secret wish with others after blowing out your birthday candles, it's forbidden to cut or break your noodles on your birthday, so cook the noodles whole instead of breaking them to fit the pot. (Guided by the same superstition, the Chinese traditionally get their hair cut before celebrations since cutting is a metaphor for shortening a life.) At banquets, a filling course of noodles or rice is traditionally served at the end of the meal so that your guests are not left hungry. By that time, I'm usually too full to eat, but I always make room for noodles on my birthday to ensure a long life.

1 pound fresh **Chinese egg noodles**

½ cup **chicken broth**

2 tablespoons **soy sauce**

1 tablespoon **chili bean paste** (*doubanjiang*)

1 tablespoon **rice vinegar**

2 teaspoons **Asian sesame oil**

1 tablespoon **vegetable oil**

1 medium **yellow onion**, sliced

2 **garlic cloves**, minced

1 1-inch knob fresh **ginger**, minced

¼ pound **snow peas** (about 1½ cups)

¼ cup chopped fresh **cilantro leaves**

Bring a large pot of water to a boil, add the noodles, and cook until they are just tender, about 2 minutes. Drain well and set aside.

In a small bowl, stir together the chicken broth, soy sauce, chili bean paste, vinegar, and sesame oil. Set aside.

In a wok, heat the vegetable oil over high heat. Add the onion, garlic, and ginger and stir-fry for 30 seconds, until fragrant. Add the snow peas and cook, stirring constantly, for 1 minute, until they are bright green. Add the chicken broth mixture and stir to coat the vegetables. Then add the noodles and toss to combine with the other ingredients. Cook for 3 to 4 minutes, until the noodles have absorbed the sauce. Turn the noodles into a serving dish and top with the cilantro.

WHOLE STEAMED FISH

SERVES 4 AS PART OF A LARGER MEAL

For the Chinese, as in many other cultures, fish plays a large role in festive celebrations. The Chinese word for fish (*yu*) is a homophone for the Chinese equivalents to "wish" and "abundance"—so serving fish symbolizes a wish for prosperity and abundance. Carp, in particular, is an important figure in Chinese mythology; legend has it that a carp could leap the falls of the Yellow River at Dragon Gate and be transformed into a mighty dragon. At banquets, fish is served whole—with both the head and the tail attached (and the head pointed toward the guest of honor)—thus connoting a good beginning and ending for the coming year. When a fish is served at a banquet, you know the meal is about to end, as it's typically the last main dish served before the rice dish and dessert.

Rinse the fish and pat it dry. Put the fish on a heatproof plate. Set a steamer basket (can be bamboo, aluminum, or even a plate placed in a larger pot) over a pan of boiling water, and set the plate in the steamer. Sprinkle the kosher salt lightly over the fish. Cover the steamer or pot and cook for 10 to 12 minutes, until the fish is cooked through and the flesh flakes easily when pierced with the tip of a knife.

A few moments before the fish has finished cooking, heat the vegetable oil in a small saucepan over medium heat until it is hot but not smoking. As soon as the fish is done, drain off any cooking liquid from the plate, and sprinkle the scallions and ginger over the fish. Immediately pour the hot oil over the top; it will sizzle and slightly wilt the scallions.

Combine the soy sauce and rice wine in a small bowl, and drizzle the mixture over the fish. Garnish with cilantro leaves and serve immediately.

1 1½-pound **whole fish** (such as sea bass or red snapper), cleaned and scaled

Kosher salt

2 to 3 tablespoons **vegetable oil**

2 **scallions** (green and white parts), thinly sliced

1 1-inch-knob fresh **ginger**, julienned

2 tablespoons **soy sauce**

1 tablespoon **Shaoxing rice wine**

Fresh **cilantro leaves**, for garnish

★ ★
TIP

Even though whole fish is must-have banquet fare, it is also everyday fare and simple to steam it at home. The key is to avoid overcooking it. Here the hot oil mixed with soy sauce is poured over the steamed fish to "cook" the garnish.

COCKTAILS

WATERMELON
SOJU PUNCH

Page 181

As chefs morph into bartenders (and vice versa), a new generation of "bar chefs" has adopted Asian flavors and ingredients. They're creating new libations by infusing the likes of Asian citrus (yuzu and Kaffir lime), preserved and salted fruits (Japanese and Vietnamese plums), and Eastern spices (*shichimi* powder and Sriracha). At the same time, traditional rice liquors like *soju*, and grain alcohol like the sorghum-distilled Chinese rocket fuel *baijiu*, are also finding their way into modern cocktails. Even classics like the Bloody Mary (see page 182) and the *michelada* (see page 188), are getting updated with Asian flavors, including kimchi, fish sauce, and *togarashi*, a Japanese spice mix. This makes sense to me, since bartenders have more of a creative license for experimentation than chefs with culinary pedigrees rooted in tradition, so cocktails provide a natural platform to expand our Asian flavor horizon.

At a recent LUCKYRICE Cocktail Feast, host "Iron Chef" Masaharu Morimoto played bartender, reminding us that Japanese mixology is leading the curve when it comes to cocktail culture, with its handcrafted spirits, artisanal mixers, and specialty carved ices. However, cocktail culture in Asia is a relatively new phenomenon, even though it's now growing by leaps and bounds. Sure, Asians have always enjoyed their drink—be it at casual Japanese gastropubs or more scandalous Vietnamese hostess bars—but instead of cocktails we've been drinking fortified distilled white spirits like Korean *soju*, Chinese *baijiu*, or brown spirits straight.

The generations before mine didn't grow up drinking gin and tonics or vodka martinis. If anything, tea was traded for beer at lunch, and shots of spirits were consumed at weddings and birthdays. Now a new generation of cocktail drinkers in Asia is embracing spirits, just as Asian flavors are invigorating classic cocktails, from New York to Tokyo to London. Here are ten Asian-inspired libations to intoxicate your palate.

WATERMELON *SOJU* PUNCH

SERVES 4

This fun drink is perfect for sharing. Simply combine watermelon with *soju*, serve it up with cocktail straws, and start slurping! Make sure your watermelon is ice-cold; it is worth the extra step to freeze some of the watermelon juice into ice cubes so that the punch is not further diluted by the water in ice cubes. *Soju*—Korea's most popular alcoholic drink—is a cheap, clear, and colorless distilled beverage made with ethanol and water. At the *pochas*, or drinking pop-up spots, in Korea (and Koreatowns across America), this punch is also served ladled into rice bowls, which I think makes perfect sense for this soup of a cocktail.

Cut the watermelon in half. You will only need half of the watermelon, so refrigerate the other half for another use. Scoop the watermelon flesh into a blender, keeping the watermelon "bowl" intact. If necessary, slice a little off the bottom of the watermelon bowl so it sits level.

In a blender, puree the watermelon. Strain the puree through a sieve. Freeze 2 cups of the strained watermelon juice into ice cubes and refrigerate the remainder of the watermelon juice. When ready to serve, pour the watermelon juice back into the watermelon half, and then top with the *soju* and ginger ale. Add the watermelon ice cubes to the bowl. Stir, and serve with 4 straws in the watermelon half or with a ladle and individual bowls on the side.

1 small **seedless watermelon**, well chilled

2 cups *soju*

1 12-ounce bottle **Bruce Cost Ginger Ale**

★ ★
TIP

You can purchase *soju* (or *shochu*, in Japanese) at most upscale wine stores.

KIMCHI BLOODY MARY AND SEAFOOD BRUNCH

SERVES 8

For a real showstopper, impress your guests at your next merry brunch gathering with a buffet of towering seafood coupled with a Bloody Mary punch bowl. I love to host brunch, which is so much more relaxed than a dinner party. I'll typically serve platters overflowing with crab claws (Alaskan crab claws are readily available, but if you can find them, Florida stone crab or California's Dungeness crab legs are sweet and sublime), poached shrimp, and freshly shucked oysters. The secret to the Bloody Mary mix is kimchi and its juice, which is also a great probiotic (and hint: a hangover remedy for Sunday mornings). Grilled *shishito* peppers add a smoky punch to this savory concoction and make for an unusual edible garnish.

PREPARE THE BLOODY MARY MIX: In a blender, combine the kimchi, Sriracha, Worcestershire sauce, rice vinegar, and tomato juice; blend for about 1 minute. Strain the blended liquid into a pitcher, and discard the solids. Season with the sea salt and black pepper. Chill in the refrigerator for at least 30 minutes.

Stir the vodka into the chilled mix, and pour the drink into tall collins glasses filled with ice; or serve in a punch bowl set over ice for guests to help themselves.

ARRANGE THE GARNISHES: Add the seafood to platters for guests to help themselves, to either add to their cocktails or to enjoy separately.

FOR THE BLOODY MARY:

2 cups **kimchi** (including as much of the liquid from the top of the jar as possible; see page 45)

2 to 3 tablespoons **Sriracha**, or more to taste

2 tablespoons **Worcestershire sauce**

2 tablespoons **rice vinegar**

6 cups **tomato juice**

1 teaspoon **sea salt**, or to taste

1 teaspoon freshly **ground black pepper**, or to taste

2 cups **vodka**

FOR THE GARNISHES:

8 **oysters**, freshly shucked, on the half shell

1 pound medium **shrimp**, cooked, peeled, and deveined

1 pound **crab claws**, cooked and with outer shells removed

Kimchi (see page 45)

Shishito **chiles**, grilled

Lemon wedges

Assorted pickled vegetables (stalks of pickled cucumbers add zest and crunch; see page 37)

AFTERNOON GIN TEA

MAKES 1 POT, SERVES 2

Gin time and tea time are both entrenched British traditions, and the pair makes quite a heady cocktail. The British colonized much of Asia, and in the process, they brought over their traditions, including a proper English tea. This cocktail picks up both citrus and smoky notes from Lapsang Souchong, a black tea that originates from the Chinese province of Fujian and is made of Lapsang leaves that have been smoked over a pinewood fire. Gin, of course, has a lurid history as the bathtub spirit of choice during Prohibition, when the homemade brew was clandestinely served in teapots as part of the afternoon ritual. For parties, I like to mull a big batch of this "tea" with Asian-forward herbs like star anise, black peppercorns, and Kaffir lime leaves. As a wink to tradition, I pour the cocktail from a teapot into teacups.

1 **star anise pod**

1 **dried Kaffir lime leaf**, crumbled

5 **whole black peppercorns**

¾ cup hot brewed **Lapsang Souchong tea** (from 1 tea bag)

1 teaspoon grated fresh **ginger**

2 tablespoons **honey**

4 ounces (½ cup) **Bombay Sapphire East gin**

Fill a small square of cheesecloth with the star anise, Kaffir lime leaf, and peppercorns; tie it closed with twine. In a teapot, combine the spice bag, hot Lapsang Souchong tea, ginger, and honey. Add the gin and stir. Serve immediately in teacups.

GREEN JUICE ELIXIR

MAKES 1 COCKTAIL

I love the taste of green juice—the less adulterated with fruit and sweet vegetables, the better. The astringency of leafy greens like kale and spinach gives me instant energy, and I prefer the drink with a zesty lemon kick and a healthy dose of fresh ginger, with its juice, for heat. If you're tiring of spinach, try substituting other greens, like chrysanthemum or tatsoi or any number of Asian leafy greens. Gin pairs well with mellow cucumbers, especially Japanese ones, which are thin-skinned, nearly devoid of seeds, and entirely edible. This strong concoction will redefine your daily green juice—just have it at 8 p.m. instead of 8 a.m.

2 cups fresh **spinach leaves**

½ **Japanese cucumber**

1 **Asian pear**, halved and cored

1 2-inch knob fresh **ginger**

1½ ounces (1 jigger) **Bombay Sapphire East gin**

1 **lemon wedge**

2 or 3 fresh **Thai basil leaves**

Using a juicer, process the spinach with the cucumber, one of the pear halves, and the ginger. Pour the mixture into a tall collins glass and add the gin. Add ice to fill the glass, and stir. Squeeze the lemon wedge over the drink, adding the juice to taste, and garnish with the Thai basil leaves and a wedge of the remaining pear.

VIETNAMESE *MICHELADA*

MAKES 1 COCKTAIL

Michelada, a traditional Mexican beer refresher spiced with hot sauce, salt, lime, and Worcestershire and served icy cold, is something I want to drink all day long in the summer. Beer is a natural complement to many Asian foods, and this beer punch carries flavors reminiscent of Southeast Asia's spicy, savory foods. It's actually surprising how similar Mexican and Vietnamese cuisines are, with their fill of limes, chiles, and umami flavors.

Togarashi **spice mix**, to taste

1 **lime wedge**

2 tablespoons fresh **lime juice**

1 dash **fish sauce**

1 squeeze **Sriracha**

1 12-ounce **dry pale lager**, such as Asahi beer

1 **star fruit**, cut into thin wedges

Chill a beer mug or pint glass in the freezer until ice-cold.

Sprinkle the *togarashi* spice mixture on a small plate. Run the lime wedge around the rim of the cold mug to dampen it, and then dip the rim into the spice mixture. Fill the mug halfway with ice, and add the lime juice, fish sauce, and Sriracha. Stir. Add the beer, leaving 1 inch at the top of the mug. Stir briefly to incorporate all the ingredients. Then top up the mug with beer, making sure not to disturb the spice rim. Garnish with a wedge of star fruit.

★ ★ NOTE This cocktail gets a kick from the *togarashi* pepper mix, best known as a topping for ramen and other Japanese goodies. You can make your own mix by blending a teaspoon of finely crushed dried red chiles with a teaspoon of salt.

SHANGHAI MULE

MAKES 1 COCKTAIL

A variation on the Moscow Mule, this cocktail travels across Eurasia to Shanghai, where vodka is traded in for *baijiu*, a strong distilled spirit that has long been the liquor of choice in China and is now making a splash in the United States. Usually made from sorghum, *baijiu*'s composition varies according to where it is produced; glutinous or sticky rice is popular in southern China, whereas the northerners (where this spirit is more widely consumed) use wheat, barley, and millet. This cocktail is traditionally served in a copper mug because copper's conductivity preserves the coldness. This is a simple drink, and it benefits from the purity and spiciness of unfiltered ginger ale, like the one from Bruce Cost, which is made with real ginger.

1½ ounces (1 jigger) **baijiu**
1 tablespoon fresh **lime juice**
½ cup **Bruce Cost Ginger Ale**
1 **lime wedge**, for garnish
1 quarter-size slice **crystallized ginger**, for garnish

Chill a copper mug.

Combine the *baijiu* and lime juice in a small cup, and pour the mixture into the mug. Add 4 standard sized ice cubes, or one specialty cocktail ice sphere, and pour in the ginger ale. Garnish the mug with the wedge of lime and crystallized ginger.

FROM TOKYO TO MANHATTAN

MAKES 1 COCKTAIL

The happy occurrence of Tokyo mixologists transplanted to Manhattan (and, along the way, intoxicating us with their cocktails) inspired this cocktail. Both of these cocktail hubs converge in this twist on a classic. Traditionally a Manhattan is made with American whiskey and served in a short glass, but my cocktail is made with a Japanese single-malt whiskey and is served in a martini glass for added merriment.

2 ounces (¼ cup) **Japanese whiskey** (preferably a single-malt, such as Suntory Yamazaki)

1 ounce (2 tablespoons) **sweet vermouth**

2 to 3 dashes **Angostura bitters**

1 **Luxardo maraschino cherry**

Fill a cocktail shaker halfway with ice, add the whiskey, vermouth, and bitters, and shake to combine. Strain the cocktail into a martini glass, and top with the maraschino cherry.

NOTE

This drink takes on an opulent note with the addition of the Luxardo maraschino cherry, an imported Italian cherry candied with marasca syrup.

COCKTAIL TONIC

MAKES 1 COCKTAIL

It's not a secret that cocktails are remedies in disguise—they've been known to cure everything from insomnia to heartache—but ingredients like digestive bitters and anti-malarial tonic water are actually the bedrock of medicinal mixology (yes, there is such a movement!). Apothecary cocktail bars have been popping up from New York to London, featuring ingredients like herbs and homeopathic extracts that not only help make delicious cocktails, but just might also heal what ails us.

In a cocktail shaker, combine the bitters and tonic water with the ginger and lemongrass. Pour into a collins glass half filled with ice cubes. Add the gin and stir to blend. I serve my cocktails with the lemongrass and ginger—along with a straw—but feel free to remove these ingredients if you soak them in the cocktail before serving.

 ★ ★ TIP

My gin of choice is Bombay Sapphire East, which contains 12 botanicals, including Vietnamese black peppercorn and Thai lemongrass, formulated for taste but also known remedies with antiseptic and antioxidant benefits.

2 dashes of **bitters**

½ cup **tonic water**

1 2-inch knob fresh **ginger**, slightly pounded

1 **lemongrass stalk** (white and light green parts), slightly pounded to release the aromatics

1½ ounces (1 jigger) **Bombay Sapphire East gin**

The elixir of the East, rice wine has brought good cheer across Asia for millennia. Since the Tang dynasty, Chinese artists have credited rice for their creativity: poets like Li Bai have waxed lyrical about the "rituals" of writing while drunk on rice and the calligrapher Zhang Xu (known as one of the Eight Immortals of the Wine Cup) would use his hair as a paintbrush while imbibing.

Like kimchi and other Asian fermented foods, rice wines are quickly making their way behind American bars. Sparkling sakes sipped like champagne and sake-laced martinis were the first to make their way onto American cocktail menus. However, today, there are plenty of spots that carry dozens of sakes as well as sophisticated cocktails blended with other rice spirits. One of my favorites is *shochu* with a touch of grapefruit and yuzu juices, topped with Kaffir lime. Today Korea's most ubiquitous spirit is *soju* (a versatile distilled spirit that can be made from various grains, including rice); it is consumed as an everyday beverage but is also brought out on special occasions. At a karaoke bar, there's seemingly a bottle of *soju* on every table, for both businessmen sealing lucrative deals and groups of karaoke-goers seeking liquid courage.

Nearly every Asian culture has its own rice wine (it's technically more like a beer because of the distillation process, but "wine" more accurately captures its personality): there's the well-known and refined Japanese sake, the sweet, amber-colored Shaoxing rice wine (indispensable for many Chinese dishes, like Shanghainese Drunken Chicken, page 168), and Korea's *makgeolli*, a traditional milky rice wine with a substantial body. Despite rice wine's long legacy and repute, it's remarkably easy to make a simple version at home with just two ingredients: rice and yeast (see page 196).

TIKI REFRESHER

MAKES 1 COCKTAIL

Recently there has been a revival of tiki cocktail culture, bringing beachy flavors like rum and coconuts back into vogue, but actually rum and coconuts have always made a great couple. Bright, frothy, and sweet, these Polynesian-inspired cocktails are born of the Hollywood imagination. Tiki cocktail culture does not actually originate from Polynesia, but is in fact a 20th-century American invention from a time when Elvis Presley starred in *Blue Hawaii* and *South Pacific* wove its way into our popular imagination. This refreshing recipe has the spirit of tiki cocktails, but is made with coconut water and no added sugar.

2 ounces (¼ cup) **golden rum**
2 ounces (¼ cup) **coconut water**

Fill a tall collins glass with ice. Combine the rum and coconut water in a small pitcher, and pour the mixture over the ice.

★ ★ TIP

If you have a fresh coconut lying around, use the water from that instead, and break the coconut into little pieces to serve on the side. Fresh coconuts can also make great serving vessels; just make sure to adjust the proportion of rum to coconut water so that the cocktail contains equal amounts of both.

HOME-BREWED RICE WINE

MAKES 2 CUPS

To make rice wine at home, all you need is rice and one special ingredient: a yeast ball, which is a mixture of microbes, fungi, bacteria, and yeasts, dried out and combined with rice flour into a ball about the size of a Ping-Pong ball.

4 cups uncooked **sweet glutinous rice**

1 **Chinese yeast ball** (available in Chinese groceries)

★ ★
NOTE

Place the rice in a bowl, add hot water to cover by 1 inch, and soak for 1 hour or as long as overnight. Drain the rice and place it in a large pot. Add 3 cups of water, bring to a boil, and cook for 15 to 20 minutes, until the rice is cooked through but not too soft; the grains should remain separate. Set the pot aside.

While the rice is cooling, crumble and sprinkle the yeast ball over the rice, and stir it in. Use a rice paddle to push the rice evenly against the sides of the pot until you have a well in the middle. Cover the pot with plastic wrap, and then place the lid over the plastic wrap. Wrap the pot in a heavy towel and place it in a warm, dark place. Let stand for about 5 days to ferment.

After 5 days, the well in the rice should be full of liquid with some light effervescence. If it's not, rewrap the pot and let it stand longer, for as long as another week—but keep in mind that as the rice continues to ferment, it will start to lose its effervescence and deepen in alcohol content and flavor. Taste the liquid as it ferments to determine when it's reached your liking.

To finish, spoon the rice into a square of cheesecloth and squeeze the liquid into a clean jar. (The fermented rice can be eaten or added to dessert soups like the *tong yuan,* see page 201.) Pour the liquid remaining in the pot into the jar, screw on a lid, and refrigerate until ready to serve, up to one month.

Depending on how long the rice wine brews, its pungency and proof will vary, moving quickly from a sweet, effervescent wine to a whiskey-like *soju.* And because it isn't pasteurized, the liquid will sour and turn into vinegar if it's left to ferment too long. Unlike wine, where the fermentation is of naturally occurring grape sugars, rice wine is made from rice starch that has been converted to sugar, so it is more akin to the process of making beer and whiskey.

SWEETS

**ALMOND "TOFU" WITH
FRUIT COCKTAIL**
Page 205

In the midst of our love affair with Asian cuisines, you might wonder why desserts haven't made more of a splash on our menus—why, for instance, green tea ice cream and fried bananas still seem to dominate dessert menus at even the most innovative Asian restaurants. And in Asia, often there is no dessert menu at all . . . just a plate of sliced oranges (and maybe some almond cookies, see page 207) with the check. Despite Asia's illustrious culinary culture, there is not much of a traditional dessert culture (though that is changing as Westernized desserts make their way into Asian cities). That's not to say that Asians don't have a sweet tooth—of course we do—but in Asia, we don't "save room" for a decadent dessert course.

Perhaps that's because sweet dishes are often incorporated into the meal itself (think sesame balls or egg tarts during dim sum) or snacked on throughout the day (as the Thai do with mango pudding). When meals do end on a sweet note, however, it's almost always with a fruit platter (see page 209) or a warm sweet soup like *tong yuan* (see opposite) with sticky rice balls stuffed with sweet red bean paste. In fact, sticky rice forms the basis of many desserts, as in the Eight Treasure Rice (an Asian fruitcake, if you will; page 214).

Asian desserts are chock-full of grains, beans, fruits, and nuts, all of which are toppings for one of my favorite treats: shaved ice (*bao bing*). The most decadent thing that goes on top is a dollop of sugar water and some condensed milk. In this chapter, I've provided recipes for a trio of icy treats that will perk you up (even without the caffeine!): *matcha* green tea unconventionally blended with coconut milk (see page 210), Vietnamese coffee with a caramel-like body (see page 213), and sugary Thai Iced Tea Pops (page 212).

At the same time, as Western lifestyles make their way into Asian culinary culture, cakes and other desserts are becoming more and more popular, especially in cities like Tokyo and Taipei, where schoolgirls line up outside coffee and dessert shops for afternoon slices of chocolate cake. As much as I love my fruit platters and shaved ice, I know the next chapter of Asian dessert culture will come with many delicious surprises.

SWEET STICKY RICE BALLS IN SOUP

Yin-Yang Tong Yuan

SERVES 4 TO 6

Tong yuan, sweet stuffed rice balls, is a popular dish during holidays such as the Lantern Festival, when round, moon-shaped foods are eaten for auspiciousness, and at weddings and other celebrations. After all, *yuan* is a homophone for the Chinese word for "reunion," symbolizing harmony and togetherness. When offered as a last course, these rice balls are frequently served in a sweet, clear soup.

Traditional Chinese *tong yuan* are typically filled with ground black sesame, but at a recent LUCKYRICE wedding banquet at Shun Lee Palace in Manhattan, chef Susur Lee experimented with adding chocolate ganache to the balls instead, for yin and yang. This East-meets-West pairing is inspired by those delicious dumplings.

6 ounces (1 cup) **semisweet chocolate chips**

⅓ cup **heavy cream**

3 tablespoons **black sesame seeds**

2 tablespoons **coconut oil**

2 tablespoons **granulated sugar**

2 cups **sweet glutinous rice flour**

¼ cup **rice flour**

¼ cup **rock sugar**

Put the chocolate chips in a mixing bowl. Heat the cream in a small saucepan until it is almost at a boil, and then pour it over the chocolate chips. Whisk together until the chocolate has melted and the mixture is smooth and glossy. Set aside for a few minutes to cool and firm up.

Using a mortar and pestle, grind the sesame seeds to a paste; you should have about 2 tablespoons. Heat the coconut oil in a small saucepan over low heat. Mix in the granulated sugar and ground sesame seeds until they are well combined. Cover and chill in the freezer while you make the dough.

For the dough, mix the two rice flours together in a bowl. Add 1 cup of water and knead for about 15 minutes, or until the dough is no longer sticky. Divide the ball of dough in half. On a flour-dusted

recipe continues

surface, divide each piece in half and shape it into a cylinder about 2 inches thick. Cut the dough into 1-inch-wide segments.

To form the rice balls, take a segment of dough and press it with your thumb to create an indentation. Place a marble-size piece of the sesame stuffing in the hollow, and close the dough around it with your fingers. Roll the dough to create a round ball, and set it aside on a flour-dusted surface. Repeat until you have used half of the dough. Follow the same procedure with the chocolate mixture for the second half of the dough.

When you are ready to cook the rice balls, fill a large pot with water and bring it to a gentle boil (a furious boil will break open the rice balls). Immerse the rice balls in the water, and cook until they expand slightly and are almost translucent, about 15 minutes. Stir occasionally to keep the rice balls from sticking to the bottom of the pot.

 Meanwhile, bring 6 cups of water to a gentle boil in a medium pot. Add the rock sugar and cook over medium heat until the liquid starts to simmer. You want to serve this dish hot, so hold the liquid at a simmer until the rice balls are ready to serve.

To serve, add rice balls (2 chocolate and 2 sesame, or more if desired) to each bowl and fill with the sweet soup.

** TIP

Uncooked rice balls can be covered
with plastic wrap and frozen for up
to a month or refrigerated for up to
a week for a later use.

ALMOND "TOFU" WITH FRUIT COCKTAIL

Xingren Doufu

SERVES 4

A popular treat on tables throughout Asia—especially at dim sum—this milky dessert can take on many consistencies: as firm, jiggly cubes, as an almost crisp and crunchy finish when made with agar-agar, or as a sweetened tofu pudding. To call this tofu is a bit misleading since my recipe uses agar-agar, not tofu, which has the texture of gelatin. A Japanese version—called *annin tofu*—is actually made with crushed apricot kernels instead of almond extract, and is delicate and delicious. Though it doesn't sound very sophisticated, canned fruit cocktail—as well as its syrup—is the perfect topping.

¼ cup **sugar**

4½ teaspoons **agar-agar powder**, or 4½ teaspoons (about 2 pouches) **gelatin**

1½ cups **whole milk**

2 tablespoons **almond extract**

1 8-ounce can **fruit cocktail in heavy syrup**, chilled

★★ TIP

For a pretty presentation, substitute some of the fruit cocktail with canned mandarin oranges. Pour the mixture into little rice bowls rather than a square dish before refrigerating.

Bring 1½ cups of water to a boil in a small saucepan, and add the sugar and agar-agar. Stir until dissolved. Pour in the milk and the almond extract, and continue stirring until the mixture is well blended. Remove from the heat.

Pour the mixture into an 8 x 8-inch square dish. Refrigerate until the dessert is starting to firm up but is not yet fully set (about 10 minutes for agar-agar, and 30 minutes for gelatin). Stir about half of the can of drained fruit cocktail into the mixture, making sure it is immersed in the pudding. Chill until set. To serve, cut the chilled pudding into 1-inch cubes and divide among 4 bowls. Top each bowl with additional fruit cocktail and its syrup.

THAI MANGO PUDDING

Khao Niaow Ma Muang

SERVES 6

Fabulous on its own, this mango pudding can also be served with sweet sticky rice, or on a banana leaf as a nod to Thailand, where this snack is eaten throughout the day. Instead of the larger, more fibrous Ataulfo mangoes, I prefer to use the little golden Manila mangoes, which have a buttery flesh with a deep yellow hue and a higher sugar content. This dessert is often created by making a rice pudding with coconut milk and serving it with fresh mangoes. I like a smoother, more decadent pudding, so I blend thicker cream of coconut with mango puree and serve it over sweet sticky rice. I like the way the pudding complements the simplicity and toothsomeness of the rice.

1 cup uncooked **sweet sticky rice**

5 ripe **Manila mangoes**, peeled and pitted

1 cup **unsweetened cream of coconut**

½ cup packed **light brown sugar**

Juice of 1 **lime**

Place the rice in a bowl, add water to cover, and soak for about 30 minutes. Then drain the rice thoroughly, and cook it according to the package directions or in a rice cooker on the sweet rice setting.

Place the mangoes in a food processor and pulse until pureed, about 1 minute. Add the cream of coconut, brown sugar, and lime juice and pulse until combined, about another minute.

To serve, place a scoop of rice (about the size of an ice cream scoop) on each plate, and mound it with a scoop of mango pudding.

GRILLED PEACHES WITH ALMOND COOKIES

MAKES 24 COOKIES, SERVES 8

If there is a signature cookie that you'll find across China, it's probably not the fortune cookie of the popular imagination, but rather the almond cookie. In Chinese American bakeries, these almond cookies are stacked high in window displays, and in Chinese American eateries, they are brought out (with oranges and the bill) at the end of the meal. My version of these almond cookies is light and nutty from the almond dough—and a little reminiscent of Italian amaretti biscuits. In the summer, when peaches are in season, I simply add peaches to the grill after I've turned it off and allow them to dawdle until they are softened, sweetened, and slightly charred.

Cooking spray to grease the baking sheets

2 cups **whole blanched almonds**, plus another 24 almonds for topping the cookies

⅔ cup **sugar**

4 teaspoons grated **lemon zest**

Dash of **sea salt**

1 large **egg**

8 ripe medium **yellow peaches**, pitted and halved

Once baked, the cookies can be stored at room temperature for about a week in a tightly sealed container.

Preheat the oven to 350°F and grease 2 baking sheets with cooking spray. Process the 2 cups of almonds in a food processor until finely ground. Add the sugar, lemon zest, sea salt, and egg and pulse about 10 times or until the dough forms a ball.

Remove the almond dough from the processor and divide it into 24 portions. Roll the portions on a lightly floured surface to form small balls. Distribute the balls on the prepared baking sheets, leaving at least an inch between them. Gently press an almond onto the center of each ball, pushing down to flatten the cookie slightly. Bake for 13 to 15 minutes, or just until the cookies are golden. Remove the baking sheets from the oven, and allow the cookies to cool on the sheets.

To grill the peaches, heat an indoor grill pan over medium heat and lightly grease the pan. Place the peaches, cut side down, on the prepared grill pan. Turn off the heat, cover the pan, and let the peaches cook for 5 to 8 minutes, until softened and slightly charred. Remove, and serve the peaches with the almond cookies.

ENDING ON A FRESH NOTE

As for many Asian families, dessert is a platter of fruit to share, something to cleanse the palate and to end the meal on a sweet, refreshing note. On most days, I'd rather have a plate of juicy sliced oranges than a rich chocolate cake—or, better yet, a platter of several sliced citrus fruits that showcase how delightfully bitter a pomelo grapefruit can taste compared to the sunny sweetness of a clementine.

The difference between mediocre supermarket fruit, bred for a long shelf life, and ripe seasonal fruit eaten at its peak of freshness is like the difference between eating to live and living to eat. Have you ever wondered why the Japanese sell perfectly perfumed and musky melon for more yen per ounce than gold? They know the value of nature at its peak.

Fruit (and vegetable) carving is a traditional craft that is practiced throughout Asia, so much so that the presentation of a fruit platter matters (almost) as much as its taste. My fruit basket is usually overflowing with whatever I've found fresh at the market in Chinatown: rambutans, clementines, star fruit, mangoes, lychees, guavas, dragon fruit, and other more tropical fruits that round out that apple a day. Have a go with that melon scooper, and experiment by cutting shapes with a good sharp paring knife, and you'll be surprised at your fruit carving mastery.

MATCHA GREEN TEA COCONUT FROZEN BARS

MAKES 6 POPSICLES

If you're a fan of Japanese green tea ice cream, try this dairy-free popsicle made with *matcha*, or green tea powder, which delivers a similar icy, milky burst of sweet and bitter. Traditional Japanese tea ceremonies center around the ritual preparation, serving, and drinking of *matcha* green tea, which—along with Zen Buddhism—was brought to Japan from China in the 12th century and continues to be popular in Zen monasteries (and nowadays way beyond Japan, thanks to the discovery of *matcha*'s culinary uses and health benefits). *Matcha* tea carries more inherent sweetness and flavor than other coarser-grade teas, but it is also intensely strong. For this frozen dessert, I use coconut milk, which isn't traditional at all but is nonetheless a fun twist on an otherwise classic flavor pairing of green tea and sweetened red beans. Canned red beans (azuki) can be found either whole, coarsely mashed, or as a smooth paste.

Holding a small fine-mesh sieve over a small bowl, use a wooden spatula to force the *matcha* powder through the sieve to break up any clumps. Whisk in ¼ cup hot water, stirring until the mixture is free of lumps. Add an additional cup of water, the coconut milk, and the sweetened red beans, and mix together until well combined. Pour the mixture into ice-pop molds and freeze for at least 5 hours.

1 tablespoon **matcha powder**

1 13.5-ounce can **coconut milk**

½ cup **whole sweetened azuki beans**, drained of any canned liquid

★ ★ TIP

If you don't have ice-pop molds, use 6-ounce plastic cups. After freezing your pops for about an hour, insert a wooden ice-pop stick or plastic spoon into each cup.

VIETNAMESE ICED
COFFEE POPS

Page 213

MATCHA GREEN
TEA COCONUT
FROZEN BARS

Page 210

THAI ICED TEA POPS

Page 212

THAI ICED TEA POPS

MAKES ABOUT 6 POPSICLES

Super-sweet and strong Thai iced tea, brewed with Ceylon tea and sweetened with condensed milk, can't really get better . . . except when it's turned into a frozen treat. At markets across Southeast Asia, the tea is "pulled" by pouring it back and forth at high heights—both to give the tea a thick frothy top and also to cool it down while thoroughly mixing it with the condensed milk. In Thailand, this drink is often sold "to go" in little plastic bags with straws, which sounds *almost* as fun as these frozen pops. The iced tea served in Thai restaurants derives its candy-like color from food coloring (oddly enough, the same shade of Number 6 yellow food dye formerly used in Kraft macaroni and cheese) to produce the bold hues that this tea is normally associated with. Just before serving, it is usually topped with evaporated milk, which gives the tea a creamy body. For popsicles, I like to pour the tea into molds almost to the top, then add a tablespoon or two of evaporated milk to create that creamy body.

6 black **Ceylon tea bags**, or ⅓ cup **loose tea leaves**

1 14-ounce can **sweetened condensed milk**

½ to ¾ cup **evaporated milk** (about half of a 12-ounce can)

Bring 2 cups of water to a boil in a saucepan. Add the tea bags or leaves, remove the pan from the heat, and steep for 5 minutes. Toss out the tea bags (or strain out and discard the leaves). Stir in the condensed milk. Pour this mixture into ice-pop molds until they are nearly filled to the top, and then top each one with a tablespoon or two of the evaporated milk. (The milk will settle into the molds as it freezes, creating a burst of milky whiteness.) Freeze until solid, at least 5 hours.

VIETNAMESE ICED COFFEE POPS

MAKES 8 POPSICLES

If you've ever had Vietnamese iced coffee, usually made with coffee that has been individually brewed with a French drip filter, then you know it's quite a contrast to the watered-down versions that often pass for iced coffee elsewhere. Unlike much of Asia, which has a stronger history of drinking tea, Vietnam developed its coffee habit (and industry as a key exporter of coffee from its many plantations in the central highlands) when it was a French colony during the 19th century. The Vietnamese who immigrated to Louisiana couldn't find the coarse-ground French roast that they were accustomed to, so they used the bold coffee and chicory blend brought there by the Acadians. I find that the bitterness of the chicory is a great foil for the sweet condensed milk; the result is so thick and sticky that the coffee takes on a caramel-like body.

2 cups **brewed strong coffee**, preferably coffee-chicory blend or good French roast, room temperature (see Note)

1 cup **sweetened condensed milk**

1 cup **heavy cream**

In a pitcher, combine the coffee with the condensed milk and cream, and whisk until evenly blended. Divide the mixture among 8 half-cups, and freeze for at least 5 hours.

** **
NOTE

You can use a traditional Vietnamese Phin filter, but a French press also works well. Just make sure the brew is strong.

EIGHT TREASURE RICE

Babaofan

SERVES 8

Like a Christmas fruitcake, this festive gift is brought to hostesses around the holidays and is studded with candied treats—which, in this Eastern adaptation, includes red bean paste and candied fruits. What goes into the Eight Treasure Rice is a matter of individual preference (and what's on hand), but do make sure to include a lucky assortment of eight since (as I note on page 174) the Chinese word for the number, *ba,* is a homophone for *fa,* which means "prosperity." Usually this dessert is molded in a large Bundt-like pan and then released onto a platter, but I think it's more precious when baked in individual cone molds where the fruits sit on top of the sticky rice like many-jeweled stars topping a Christmas tree.

Rinse the glutinous rice well in a colander under cold running water. Place the drained rice in a saucepan, add 1½ cups of cold water, and bring to a boil over high heat. Then cover the pan, reduce the heat to very low, and cook for 30 minutes, until the rice is almost completely cooked.

Remove the pan from the heat and stir in the brown sugar and butter. If the rice is very dry, stir in a little more water to make it creamier. Set aside. Fill a deep steamer pot with a few inches of water, insert the steamer basket, and bring the water to a boil.

While the water is heating, butter the inside of 8 small, individual-serving cone molds or a large Bundt pan. Press the candied fruit onto the buttered sides of the molds, forming a decorative pattern, if desired. Spoon half of the rice into the molds, and then spread the bean paste on top. Add the remaining rice and smooth the surface with the back of a spoon. Cover the bottom of each

1½ cups uncooked **sweet glutinous rice**

2 tablespoons **dark brown sugar**

2 tablespoons **unsalted butter**, plus more for buttering the molds

1½ cups chopped **candied Chinese fruits**, such as mandarin orange slices, winter melon, cherries, dates, kumquats, lychees, ginger, and/or plums

½ cup **red bean paste**

⅓ cup **granulated sugar**

1 teaspoon **cornstarch**

Grated zest and juice of 1 **lemon**

mold tightly with aluminum foil. Set the molds in the steamer basket, cover, and steam at a simmer for 1 hour.

While the molds are steaming, whisk the granulated sugar and cornstarch together in a small saucepan set over medium heat. Whisking constantly, drizzle in 1 cup of water, stirring until smooth. Cook over medium heat for 5 to 6 minutes, until the sauce thickens. Stir in the lemon zest and juice; then remove from the heat and set aside.

Remove the molds from the steamer, and let cool slightly (about 5 minutes) before unmolding each one onto an individual plate. Pour some of the zesty syrup around each one, and serve.

PERSIMMON CAKES WITH OSMANTHUS FLOWERS

MAKES 20 CAKES

My mother has a persimmon tree in her Bay Area backyard that takes all year to bear fruit—but then the fruit ripens so quickly that we're always left with far more persimmons than we can consume before they spoil. This fruit comes in two basic types: the Fuyu, which is hard and can be eaten like an apple, and the Hachiya, the honey-sweet varietal that must be eaten only when the fruit is so ripe, it's about to burst from the skin. Thanks to my mother's bounty, I learned how to pan-fry persimmon cakes, a popular street food delicacy in China.

Mash the persimmons in a bowl. Mix in the flour bit by bit, and then knead until the consistency resembles bread dough: tacky but not sticky. (If the persimmons are small, you may need to add 1 to 2 teaspoons of water.) Cover the dough and let it rest for a couple of hours.

Toast the sesame seeds and walnuts in a dry skillet over medium-high heat. Let them cool, then grind them in a food processor. Add the osmanthus flowers, sugar, and melted butter, and pulse until well blended. On a lightly floured surface, roll out the dough to about a 1-inch thickness, and use a biscuit cutter to cut out 3-inch-wide coins. Flatten the coins and put 2 teaspoons of the filling in the center of each one. Pinch the sides up and over the filling, patting to shape it flat.

Heat the vegetable oil in a skillet over medium heat. In batches, fry the cakes, turning them over once, until they are golden brown on both sides, 4 to 5 minutes total. Remove from the skillet, sprinkle with a little sugar on top. Serve hot, or store them in an airtight container at room temperature for up to a week.

3 ripe **Hachiya persimmons**, peeled

4 cups **all-purpose flour**

6 tablespoons **black sesame seeds**

6 tablespoons **walnuts**

1 tablespoon **dried osmanthus flowers**

¼ cup **sugar**, plus more for sprinkling

3 tablespoons **unsalted butter**, melted

3 tablespoons **vegetable oil**

★ ★ NOTE

To bring out the honey of the fruit, I've added osmanthus flowers, which can be found in the dried tea and herb sections of most Asian groceries. This fragrant flower is a sweet symbol of love and romance, and is often served at Chinese wedding banquets, either mixed and brewed with green tea, sprinkled onto sweet dessert soups (like *tong yuan*, page 201), or as an addition to cakes like these, which I like to have with afternoon tea.

The recipes in this book are designed to be mixed and matched, to suit your palate and whimsy, whether you're making Sunday supper for the family or hosting a dim sum brunch. My favorite way to enjoy these menus is to throw parties for groups of 8 or more; after all, a feast is meant for sharing and eating communally is central to eating Asian-style. For inspiration, I've compiled 10 feasts for brunch, picnics, dinners, or soirées, along with cocktail pairings. If you're entertaining, cocktails are a spirited way to kick off each of the feasts, but you can also batch them ahead of time so that guests can help themselves throughout the meal.

★ **A Sichuanese Dinner Party**
Home-style fare with bold and spicy flavors

> Double-Boiled Chicken Soup
> Dandan Noodles
> Spicy Fish Stew
> *Ma Po* Tofu
> Sichuanese Chicken Wings
> Perfect Steamed Rice
> Fresh fruit platter
> TO DRINK: Shanghai Mule

★ **A Thai Gathering**
A crowd-pleaser that can be served buffet-style

> Festive Thai Leaf Wraps
> Thai Shrimp Boil and Soup
> Issan-style Pork
> Thai Grilled Beef Salad
> Thai Green Curry Coconut Mussels
> Perfect Steamed Rice
> Thai Mango Pudding
> TO DRINK: Vietnamese *Michelada*

★ **A Korean Sunday Supper**
Hearty fare for sharing, especially when the weather turns chilly

> Instant Kimchi
> Seafood *Soondubu* with Kimchi
> Kimchi Pancakes
> Grilled Korean Short Ribs
> Bibimbap
> Korean Seaweed Soup
> Perfect Steamed Rice
> TO DRINK: Watermelon *Soju* Punch

★ **A Summer Barbecue**
Finger-licking favorites for the backyard or poolside

> Hawaiian Tuna Poke
> Asian Gazpacho
> Barbecued Squid-on-a-Stick
> Beef Satay
> Grilled Chicken *Tsukune* Sausage
> Grilled Sticky Rice-on-a-Stick
> Assorted frozen pops: Vietnamese Iced Coffee, *Matcha* Green Tea Coconut, and Thai Iced Tea
> Grilled Peaches with Almond Cookies
> TO DRINK: Watermelon *Soju* Punch

★ A Classic Chinese Banquet
A festive celebration worthy of special occasions

Shanghainese Drunken Chicken

Long Life "Supreme" Broth

Whole Steamed Fish

Lion's Head Meatballs with Napa Cabbage

Chairman Mao's Red-Braised Pork Belly

Garlicky Stir-Fried Pea Sprouts

Longevity Noodles

Sweet Sticky Rice Balls in Soup

TO DRINK: Home-Brewed Rice Wine

★ A Dim Sum Brunch
An unconventional take on brunch (add a game of mahjong for extra fun)

Savory Rice Balls

Turkey Congee

Steamed Turnip Cakes

Classic Chinese Dumplings

Chrysanthemum and Tofu Salad

Grandma Hsiang's Chinese Tamales

Almond "Tofu" with Fruit Cocktail

TO DRINK: Afternoon Gin Tea

★ An All-Star Chinese Potluck Lunch
A bring-anywhere spread that will please just about anyone

Hot and Sour Soup

Jewish Pastrami Egg Rolls

Spicy Pork Noodles

ABC Beef with Broccoli

Garlicky Stir-Fried Pea Sprouts

Perfect Steamed Rice

Eight Treasure Rice

TO DRINK: Tiki Refresher

★ A Malaysian Supper
An adventurous, spicy dinner party

Herbal Bone Tea Soup

Malaysian Okra with Shrimp Paste

Sambal Stingray

Curry in a Hurry

Indonesian Fried Rice

Thai Mango Pudding

TO DRINK: Green Juice Elixir

★ A Japanese Gastropub Cocktail Soiree
Late-night snacks and cocktails (Karaoke machine recommended)

Spiced Lotus Root Chips

Grilled Sardines in Soy Sauce

Octopus with Wasabi

Fiery Edamame with Garlic Miso

Hawaiian Tuna Poke

Garlicky Smashed Cucumber Pickles

Seaweed with Cucumber and Daikon Ribbons

Japanese Fried Chicken

DIY Sushi Hand Rolls

TO DRINK: Any number of drinks would work well here, but greet your guests upon arrival with a cocktail like a Shanghai Mule or From Tokyo to Manhattan.

★ A Breezy Afternoon Picnic
Blanket-ready fare for a lazy afternoon in the park (cherry blossoms optional)

Fiery Edamame with Garlic Miso

Japanese Fried Chicken

Tea-Smoked Eggs

Vietnamese Banh Mi

Persimmon Cakes with Osmanthus Flowers

Grilled Sticky Rice-on-a-Stick

TO DRINK: Chilled sake

ACKNOWLEDGMENTS

I don't know which I love more: writing or cooking. The opportunity to share both stories and feasts in a cookbook makes me wonder if there is indeed a pot of gold at the rainbow's end. For double the happiness, I was blessed with two sparkling editors at Clarkson Potter: Jessica Freeman-Slade, who initially came to me with the idea of turning the LUCKYRICE Festivals into a book; and later Angelin Borsics, who mentored me and was my partner throughout this journey.

I am indebted to the world-class professionals at Clarkson Potter: Aaron Wehner, Rica Allannic, Doris Cooper, Danielle Deschenes, Cathy Hennessy, Phillip Leung, Natasha Martin, Kevin Sweeting, Michael Nagin, Kathie Ness, and Pam Krauss—all of whom I admire and have learned so much from. To my agent, Angela Miller, a treasure trove of knowledge and helpful advice, who stuck with me through both the ebullience and the tears.

I am in awe of the creative team responsible for the luminous images in this book: notably the visionary photographer Christina Holmes (I was smitten from the moment I saw her photography), the affable and brilliant food stylist Eugene Jho (who can turn a knob of ginger into a sculpture), and prop stylist Kalen Kaminski (who brought an inimitable fashion sensibility to every photo). Thank you to Noah Fecks and Cristina Vasquez, both ultra-talented long-time collaborators of mine, for contributing their creative vision, and to David Bowers, for enthusiastically testing the recipes.

To my team at LUCKYRICE, especially Barbara Roan, who has been my rock. She is supersmart, loyal, and a pleasure to work with. I couldn't have built LUCKYRICE without her, let alone find the time to write this book.

LUCKYRICE would not exist were it not for the chefs on our culinary council who enthusiastically joined when the festival was just a lofty idea: Andy Ricker, Anita Lo, Charles Phan, Daniel Boulud, David Chang, Eric Ripert, Floyd Cardoz, Jean-Georges Vongerichten, José Andrés, Marcus Samuelsson, Masaharu Morimoto, Pichet Ong, Sang Yoon, Susur Lee, Tadashi Ono, Zak Pelaccio, and many others. Lisa Ling, thank you for not only writing the foreword to my book and for your decades of friendship, but also for shaping the world our daughters will grow up in through the power of your voice.

And to my dearest friends and family—the ones who have said "there is no need to thank," and for whom "thank you" would never be enough. *Xie Xie.*

—— DANIELLE CHANG ——

is the founder of the **LUCKYRICE** festival, a national celebration of Asian cultures and cuisines that has taken place in more than seven cities, including New York, Los Angeles, and Chicago. She is also the host and creator of *Lucky Chow,* a PBS series about Asian food culture in America. Born in Taipei, Danielle lives with her family in New York.

INDEX

NOTE Page references in *italics* indicate photographs.

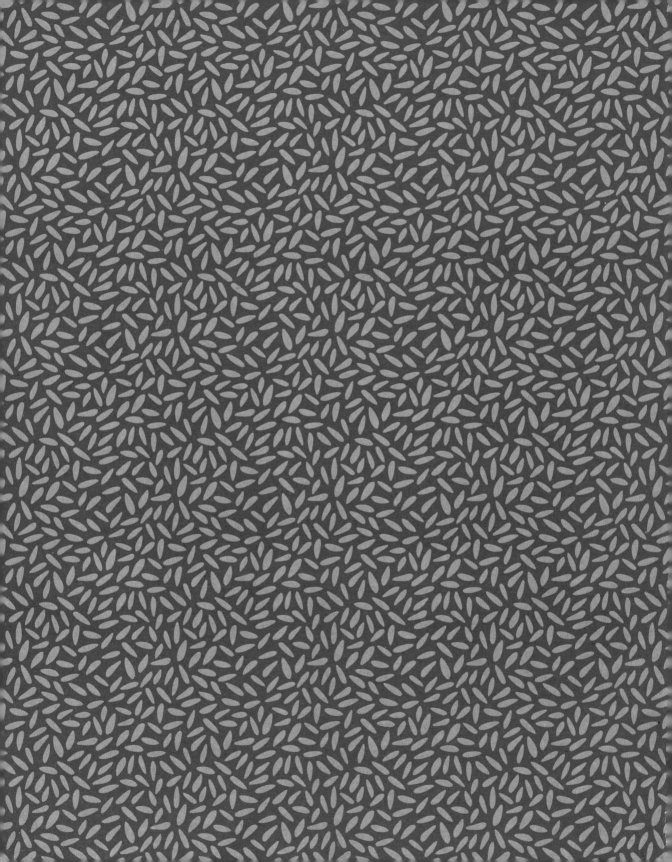